Signs of the City –
Metropolis Speaking

jovis

Signs of the City – Metropolis Speaking

Edited by Stefan Horn, Rudolf Netzelmann & Peter Winkels

Content

Open the House

Collaborations between Odd Couples

Peter Winkels,
Next Intercultural Projects, education and outreach programmes
on behalf of the House of World Cultures

An international youth project has now, for the first time, become a catalyst for workshops, exhibitions, conferences and an internet platform, which addresses the arts and the academic circuit in equal measure. Signs of the City had the potential to open the eyes of arts institutions and universities alike to the perspectives of young people on the European metropolis and beyond. The young participants were not research objects; they became authors in their own right, directly involved in the production of knowledge. Among other factors, this was achieved through unprecedented close collaboration between arts institutions, cultural agents, research centres, art galleries – large and small – and artists. Allow me a couple of remarks on one of these odd but successful couples: the artistic and organisational backbone of the project, urban dialogues, and the House of World Cultures, which has been on board since the very beginning of this journey.

The project started for me in 2005, when Stefan Horn and I met in a small community centre in Berlin-Kreuzberg, which was run by urban dialogues. We had both just finished projects on the readability of signs in big cities. I was working for the House of World Cultures on education and outreach programmes, and Stefan Horn, with his colleagues from urban dialogues, was working on applying artistic strategies to the development of economically challenged neighbourhoods in Berlin. I had produced *CityScape* together with the House of World Cultures, the Institute for Art in Context in Berlin, and the Department of Design in Education at the Polytechnic University of Hong Kong. Stefan had just finished the *Archive of Signs*, an art and education project using photography that already contained some of the major elements that were later to make up Signs of the City. We discovered that we shared many interests: we both worked with young people and artists on issues of urban life, on the visual *landscape/cityscape* of our environment, and on an image-based intercultural exchange and dialogue. However, we were also aware of the shortcomings of our two projects. *CityScape*, despite its educational and artistic power, remained within the narrow sphere of art, while the *Archives of Signs* could not reach out beyond the borders of community art. Since then, urban dialogues has worked hard to broaden the base for a more comprehensive project on signs in cities. One and a half years later, we were able to convince the new director of the House of World Cultures, Bernd M. Scherer, to join the emerging European network of Signs of the City.

While Alison Rooke praises Signs of the City in her evaluation report (see chapter 6) for the collaboration between established institutions of contemporary art or academic research and smaller cultural agents working at grass-roots level, a closer look at the intersections between these different spheres of cultural production might prove productive. A good example is the cooperation between the House of World Cultures, which is financed by the Federal Government, is situated in the midst of the government district in Berlin, engages forty to sixty employees and freelancers, and attracts more than 100,000 visitors a year, and urban dialogues, a small urban arts organisation that depends exclusively on project money and the creativity of its associates. Let me focus on three issues that nevertheless link the two: firstly, the interest in the new role of images within globalised cultural production; secondly, the need for interdisciplinary approaches in the research and exhibition of this production; and thirdly, the acceptance of participatory and outreach practices.

Time and time again, the programme of the House of World Cultures addresses the question of imagery in an age of globalisation; we explore the cultural conditions under which images are produced and interpreted. We have done so in a wide range of formats, from exhibitions like *Portrait Africa* on the history of African photography and its contemporary legacy in 2002, to *China − between past and present* on the role of photography in China since the 1950s. We have also organised international conferences on »Migrating Images« and we have examined the political ramifications of the *iconic turn*, in symposiums such as »Frames of Viewing« in 2003 or »War on Images« in 2005.

In combining exhibition practices and academic reflection, the House developed a kind of atlas of these migrating images. However, we generally remained within the sphere of high art production and academic research. New democratisation within image production, osmotic processes between street art and more elitist art scenes, and rapid technical changes often failed to find a way into the House of World Culture. The concept of Signs of the City – artistic research on the possibilities of visual literacy with an intercultural approach – was therefore very interesting to us. What could an institution of contemporary art and culture learn from a project that seemed to jump head-first into the proliferation of images, rejecting the common rejectionist evocations of a »flood of pictures« and of the cultural dangers of new media? Using a sophisticated Web 2.0 platform not only as a tool of exchange and dialogue but also as a curatorial device, Signs of the City answers the democratic promise of photography and the internet, and at the same times challenges the curatorial practises of art institutions. As a partner, Signs of the City was able to bridge the common and the elitist and to crack open »white cube« arts production. Furthermore, it opened the House to artistic productions that otherwise do not leave cyberspace. In so doing, it has added to the vast material of images and to the discourses that the House has collected throughout its history.

Signs of the City deployed some interesting strategies to cope with these vast quantities of material; these are laid out in more detail later on in this book. For now, let me just focus on the interdisciplinary approach it took and how it fused with the strategies of the House.

The House of World Cultures has always insisted on the exceptional status of art in intercultural dialogue. We have always tried to avoid functionalistic approaches to art. Artists from all over the world could trust that they would not be instrumentalised as mere decorations for conceptual frameworks designed by politicians, sociologists, or cultural scientists. We have thus been able to trigger real interdisciplinary dialogues between artists, scientists, and the public. Within our educational work in particular, we have always made it crystal clear that the artists working in the programmes were not educators or trainers, but worked as professionals in their fields. Working with artists and young people in art projects is always a process of negotiation and not of classroom teaching.

This is where I see the strongest link between the work of the House of World Cultures and Signs of the City. The project succeeded in providing a field of interdisciplinary exchange because nobody involved in the process was forced into anything but his or her profession. At the conference »Signs of the European City«, for instance, the attending academic scholars did not just take the project as raw material for their deliberations; they communicated with the artists, who were present. Similarly, the workshops were not playing grounds for artists' vanities; they became places of negotiation between students and professionals. The exhibition in the House of World Cultures incorporated appeals for audience participation – virtual and haptic alike. And, last but not least, the book you hold in your hands is an invitation to play the games of choice, comparison and communication that we so happily experienced with Signs of the City over the last two years. Art can only play a substantial role in interdisciplinary dialogues if it has strong allies to defend its autonomy. The House of World Cultures is such an important ally.

Of course, beyond the interdisciplinary description of a global visual landscape lies the pressing question of power. Therefore, the House has always contested pictorial representation practices in European cultural institutions. It did so by inviting non-European curators and artists, such as Jack Persekian, Okwui Enwesor, Wu Hung or Ackbar Abbas. Sometimes our

visitors were puzzled by the lack of so-called authentic or traditional imagery coming from the Middle East, Africa, or China.
Contrary to viewers' expectations, the display of the image
production of these cultures showed them as contemporaries,
sharing with Europeans the same global stack of images. The
appearance of non-European artists as authors in their own
right, presenting themselves not as mere victims of globalisation, but as true global cultural players, made it interesting for
our public. Participation and ownership are as important within the art system as they are in politics and social debates.

However, does it help in the face of more structural power
that the technique-driven proliferation of seemingly bound-
less image production applies? To a big cultural institution, the
mere speed of this technical development can have a slow-mo-
tion effect. Curatorial responses can either take the form of a
snap-shot, or they can throw a belated glance at changing media production. Recent waves of democratising and commer-
cialising image production – labelled Web 2.0 – particularly
demand new approaches of reflection and curating.

One strategy to narrow the gap between image technology
and reflection on images is to invest in participatory projects.
Participatory in the case of the House of World Cultures calls
for a two-way approach. On the one hand, it means inviting
people who are usually cut off from the art world as a result
of language and social segregation, to become part of artistic
production. On the other, it means learning from the cultural
practices of such people for institutional development. Collaborative art projects between young people and professional
artists are one specific tool with which to bring about this exchange of perspective and experience. What we began with the
Black Box Exercise in 2000 (learning from Chinese artists from
Hong Kong that art has its own obligation to teach art to the public), and what we developed further between 2001 and 2004,
again in collaboration with Hong Kong, in our *City-Scape* pro-

ject (learning about the power of art in producing knowledge
about the visual landscape of our cities), has now reached a
climax in the collaboration with Signs of the City.

The most important revenue you receive once you start to
get serious about participation is learning. If you succeed, none
of the *odd couples* leave the project unchanged. More than
300 young people have contributed to the ongoing discussions
about the future of globalisation, its effect on our perception
of images, our cities, and our lives. It is now up to the arts institutions – like the House of World Cultures – to look at the
material and learn from their future audience. It's up to you to
find in this book the creativity, effort, and joy that were shared
in this project.

Signs of the City – Metropolis Speaking

Stefan Horn,
Artistic Director, urban dialogues, Berlin

The city is an ocean of signs. In our modern, urban society, we are surrounded by a culture of glittering signs and images: commercial and political hoardings, private messages, spontaneous markings, bombastic graffiti and penetrating advertising, rules and regulations that seek an audience.

CITIES

Signs of the City – Metropolis Speaking was a fifteen-month youth art project that engaged with the signs of the European city by researching four metropolises and their different cultural imprints. London: the centre of Europe's biggest conurbation with its multicultural flair. A rich social fabric made up of a multitude of languages and customs, it is the heterogeneity of London, that attracts and fascinates visitors and inhabitants while at the same time offering continuous challenges. Barcelona: currently the most prospering city in Western Europe, a pivotal point between Catalan and Spanish particularities. It is a place, in which the transformation from an industry and trade-based city to a modern metropolis built on services and tourism is particularly noticeable. Berlin: a city that could, and had to, re-invent itself after the Fall of the Berlin Wall in 1989. Sometimes resembling a peaceful urban island, it is an increasingly attractive and vibrant new capital, which also however faces the challenges involved in integrating two different social and value systems. And last, but certainly not least, Sofia: the capital city of one of the youngest members of the European Union. Sofia is rapidly evolving as a melting pot and destination for many people from all over Bulgaria in search of work and prosperity – and is thus exemplary of many urban centres in Southeastern Europe.

PRE-HISTORY

Signs of the City was initiated and coordinated by the Berlin urban arts association urban dialogues, which has been producing innovative arts and culture projects at the interface of urbanity, education, and participation for the past ten years.

In Autumn 2003, urban dialogues carried out a pilot project called *Archive of Signs – Inventory of a Metropolis*. During this pilot phase, professional artists worked together with young people from social training centres in order to create an inventory and archive of the signage systems of Berlin. The results of the project were exhibited in January and February 2004 on the platforms and publicity hoardings of a Berlin tube station. Nearly half a million passersby engaged *en passant* with the photographs and collages of this public exhibition.

RESEARCH

Employing digital cameras and GPS-receivers, young people between twelve and twenty-five explored the signage systems of their cities and thus documented their urban lives. Between November 2007 and October 2008, nearly 300 young participants from Berlin, Barcelona, London and Sofia investigated their urban environment photographically, guided and accompanied by thirty professional artists in over thirty workshops. These workshops were coordinated by Watermans in London, Artibarri in collaboration with Hangar in Barcelona, the Atelier for Free Associations in Sofia, and urban dialogues in collaboration with Next Interkulturelle Projekte in Berlin. These workshops created a multifaceted view on the four cities: an interior view on urban public space from the perspective of young city dwellers. Rather than collecting coincidental snap-shots, however, this visual research was carried out on the basis of the conceptual blueprints and creative learning techniques developed by the artists.

UNDERSTANDING MY IMAGE

A core objective of the project was to impart skills in the handling of images, such as their description and interpretation. To see and perceive the world are mainly automatic processes operated by our sensory system. Within the first few months of a child's life, it develops the faculty for sight, learns how to distinguish between light and dark, and then begins to understand how to literally grasp objects spatially. One cannot *not see* (except in cases of blindness, of course). On closer scrutiny, however, this ability to see is a rather ambivalent affair, as what we perceive is already semantically marked; it therefore needs to be understood and interpreted in context. Today's world is more than ever dominated by images, and their already overwhelming presence is, if anything, on the increase. We are socialised through images; they imprint themselves on our memories; they epitomise significant moments of our personal and collective history in a media-based world. In this context, it is peculiar that the corresponding skills – how to manage and deal with images in an emancipated way – are not taught consistently. Our education systems show us how to make best use of words; they aim to convert the infant (from Latin *infans*: »one who does not (yet) speak«) into a verbally competent person. This kind of instruction and learning takes place throughout school and college education. Yet the language of signs is not given equal attention. How can we learn to use images meaningfully, to understand and also, perhaps, to be wary of them? In the tradition of an *iconic turn*, Signs of the City sought to encourage young people to engage closely with images and photographs, to scrutinize and interrogate them: What perspective has been chosen? What elements are prevalent in the image? What does the producer of the image want to express with it?

Signs of the City consciously deployed the high-speed medium of digital photography, which usually creates an excess of images: a downright pictorial congestion. All too often, the experience of digital photography ends with the moment of photographic exposure. Often, the images are not even consciously looked at afterwards. They moulder and decay on USB sticks and hard drives. The digital image, in comparison to analogue photography, is radically devalued here. Arguably, however, if we combine techniques of observing, describing and interpreting images, we may convey to young people how to grasp and comprehend images – a process that has often (and rather infelicitously) been called »visual alphabetisation«. Visual competence would perhaps be more precise. Signs of the City – Metropolis Speaking explores these questions through active and critical engagement with visual signs and images. To attain visual competence is not exclusively reserved for art historians; everybody should have the opportunity to further their visual literacy.

UNDERSTANDING MY CITY

The city as a cultural achievement of humanity is made up of a myriad of segments and stories. Millions of individuals live with or rather next to each other in cities: they represent a conglomerate of the most diverse partial interests and personal needs. They encounter each other permanently, in abstract form and *en passant*. They meet on the underground, in cars, and in theatres as much as in supermarkets. They share water, electricity and a transport system. From the three million inhabitants of Berlin, I may know around a thousand by name; I believe to be on familiar terms with around 300. I probably really only know thirty.

Through its photographic explorations, Signs of the City strove to make the participants aware of their everyday usage of the urban environment. What does my city look like? What kind of image of my city would I want to show to others (my workshop colleagues, my arts instructor, my family, and friends)? What is it I want to tell them? How can I *read* my city and capture what I have perceived in a photograph? This exercise of translation – translating an internal engagement with the city into an externalised image – is the actual core competence of the participating artists. It is in this act of translation and on the basis of their professional experience that they can support the ideas of the participants and the significance of their images, as well as their photographic practice.

This practice creates an internal view of the city. It is a form of rediscovering the city through the still images of urban photography that are generated by a young generation of city dwellers, who would or could not relinquish the city as their main habitat. The city is their *destiny*, offering many opportunities yet harbouring challenges and even disadvantages. One of the main tasks that the participating artists were therefore faced with was to bring this complexity of the metropolis to the foreground, to make it an object of discussion.

MY IMAGE IN URBAN SPACE

Digital image files nowadays contain a whole range of detailed information, that often has nothing to do with the actual image the photographer composed at the moment of exposure. A so-called EFIX-file allows the observer to glean additional information from an image, such as details on focal distance, camera model, date of exposure, shutter speed, camera aperture, photo-sensitivity, and colour profile. This is data that is defined prior to the exposure of an image: the EFIX-file is a kind of making-of that documents the generation of the digital image.

By deploying geo-position technology, photography may be enriched with very interesting additional information – namely the place where the picture was taken. Participants take so-called GPS-loggers on their photographic journeys, which allow them to track their movements. Afterwards, the geo-po-

sitional data produced by these devices can be added to any individual picture using specialised software. This image can then be opened in combination with a freely available online cartography service, such as Google Maps.

What in the first instance may seem like a redundant technical feature adds, on closer inspection, a whole new dimension to urban digital photography. Within a *youth arts* project in particular this opens up a range of playful possibilities. The image receives anchorage and feeds back to the city, to the street corner, to the place of its origin. Digital photography is infused with a new kind of physical experience, in which place and time are conjoined.

But there is more: with the help of Google Maps or other online cartography tools, the city can also be turned into a surface. The city can become a sort of *message board*, composed of news and announcements. As I move through the city, I become the felt tip pen, the quill or pencil myself, and I use the virtual view of the city to write my own messages into it.

MY CITY AS AN ASSEMBLY KIT OF IMAGES

Signs of the City by no means sought to instruct the young participants in linguistic semiotics, nor to provide them with abstract definitions as to how signs are produced and constituted. Rather, it took a much simpler idea as its starting point; that a sign represents something, which stands for something else.

Some of the workshops looked into how signage systems, which we find all over our cities, both create and bestow meaning. Pictograms and symbols, logos and emblems, but also the more subversive signs of a city, such as graffiti and tags, stickers and cut-outs, can be read as the *visual grammar* of a city. They became the real objects of examination in Signs of the City.

Many of the countless messages and signs that surround the city dweller, at least indirectly, contain instructions on how to act; they do not represent an ideal communicative situation that would allow for dialogue or feedback from the receiver. Communication only takes place, when the receiver can also become a sender, if he or she can respond. In the private or domestic spheres, this one-sided messaging takes place via radio and TV.

Graffiti and street art culture in contemporary big cities is often understood as a protest to this unilateral and thus deformed relationship in public and mass media, in which people receive more messages than they are able or allowed to send. However, it is particularly when engaging with the topic of graffiti – the (seemingly) subversive signs of the city – that young people are generally happy to take on basic principles of communication and to pay attention to the complexity of urban signage systems. How and where is such protest articulated? Where have clever marketing strategists turned the originally subversive nature of graffiti into a perfect advertising platform? To confront and read the many-sided signage systems of the city gives young people the very hands-on opportunity to discover and learn about communication models, which may be of great use to them as they become skilled at deciphering the world.

The artists participating in the project were asked to develop ideas and concepts, which would allow the point of views of the young participants on their urban environments to become visible. The resulting images serve as a point of departure for a discourse that takes place both within and outside of the project proper. The participants could this both enhance their visual competences and further develop their skills regarding the *readability* of the city.

DIVERSITY

In early October 2007, two-thirds of all participating artists met at the House of World Cultures in Berlin for an Arts and Education Lab. It was an open discussion on the content, methodologies, and aims of the workshops that were to be carried out during the year to come. It soon became apparent that the conditions for creating youth and participatory arts projects were radically different in all four cities. Nor did the range of experiences and backgrounds of the participating artists lend itself to standardisation. On the contrary, the very appeal of this project was that it allowed a whole range of approaches to be put into practice. The four workshops I will briefly sketch out below should give us an insight into this methodological diversity; for more detailed descriptions, see also chapter 1.

MY CITY

The London artist Melissa Bliss worked with young homeless people in central London. She met the participants in the morning at a welfare centre, which serves as a meeting point for the homeless. They then spent one day wandering through the city, discovering their points of view on the city in which they lived, and initiating a discussion among them about the urban environment they lived in.

MAPPING

The Berlin-based photographer and graphic designer Martin Ruge worked on developing a map of Berlin signs once a week with students from a sixth form college specialising in communication and media technologies. With the help of GPS-loggers, the participants could map the places and sites where their individual photographs were taken on an online cartography service. Thus, they created a small archive of emblems, street art, traffic signage, and other icons.

DIALOGUE

Campbell Works, an artist duo from North East London, spent one week working with deaf-mute students from the Wilhelm-von-Türk secondary school in Potsdam (near Berlin). They used pinhole cameras and a mobile dark room in public space to produce results which, spectacularly reminiscent of the early days of photography, were later digitalized. In the five-day workshop, the young participants were taken on a journey through the history of photography. They also took part in a double intercultural dialogue: one between deaf students and hearing artists and one between British artists and German participants. Every day, the group negotiated questions of communication, interpretation, and interaction.

SIGNS

For eight weeks, the Munich-based photographer Andréas Lang investigated the former industrial area of Poble Nou in Barcelona, once called the »Mediterranean Manchester«, with a group of young Barcelona city dwellers. The quarter, a veritable jigsaw puzzle between old and new, allowed the group to observe the transformations and concurrent displacement processes taking place in post-industrial urban environments – from Jean Nouvel's creation of a new urban symbol to the remnants of a former factory building. The artist sought to encourage the young participants (aged between fourteen and sixteen) to discover and discuss these transformation processes, and to photographically document their own views on them. The results were *inner landscapes* expressing the artistic engagement of the young people with their own neighbourhood.

THE LAB2 EXCHANGE PROGRAMME

The so-called LAB2, a five-day meeting of twenty-five young participants from the four cities, who were accompanied by ten artists, took place in October 2008 in Barcelona. The last four workshops of the overall project Signs of the City took place within this framework. Together, the young people from the different cities explored the city of Barcelona, and sought to work out the differences and similarities between this and the other three cities, from which they came. Despite all the possibilities provided by modern-day communication technologies, the immediacy of human encounter remains of central importance to communication and interaction. No other form of communication or dialogue is comparable to the power of physical encounters. The experiences of this nearly week-long exchange programme only served to confirm this assumption.

THE WEBSITE

The results of all workshops were immediately published on the online image database www.citipix.net. All images, the corresponding workshops, and authors, can be found and searched for there. Furthermore, guest visitors can playfully interact with the photographs by selecting and grouping five individual images into an image stripe. These interactions can then be saved onto the site. Through these features, the site seeks to offer a visual and playful level of communication that does not rely on any particular language. The platform is foremost a database, which offers the opportunity to compare and relate the images within. But it should not be confused with common Web 2.0 applications, which mainly provide language-based communication tools for members of a community.

Exhibitions

Four virtually simultaneous exhibitions in autumn 2008 put the artistic results of the project on a different form of public display. Through a wide range of formats and curatorial designs, they demonstrated the diversity of artistic approaches and the different perceptions of the young participants. The exhibitions took place at Watermans Gallery in London from 4 October to 2 November, at the House of World Cultures in Berlin from 26 September to 2 November, at Can Basté in Barcelona from 9 October to 8 November, and at Sofia's House of Cinema from 15 October to 15 November.

Conferences

The fifteen-month long project Signs of the City – Metropolis Speaking culminated in an interdisciplinary conference entitled »Signs of the European City,« hosted by the House of World Cultures Berlin on 17 - 18 October 2008. Furthermore, two one-day seminars were held in London on 4 October 2008 and in Sofia on 24 October 2008, each organised in cooperation with and hosted by the local Goethe Institutes. All three events reflected on the implications and results of this European youth arts project (see chapter 5 for a selection of papers presented at these events). The project was accompanied throughout and evaluated by the Centre for Urban and Community Research (CUCR), Goldsmiths College, University of London.

A Network as an Artwork

The individual project elements of Signs of the City – Metropolis Speaking generated a border-crossing interplay linking and engaging renowned contemporary arts institutions, media training centres, youth art and leisure organisations, and a leading academic institute for social research. Apart from urban dialogues in Berlin, the organisers of the project were Watermans and the Centre for Urban and Community Research in London, as well as Hangar in Barcelona. In Berlin, the project was carried out in cooperation with Next Interkulturelle Projekte and the House of World Cultures. All project participants were joined and interlinked at different levels in what ended up being a nodal point of innovative technology, conceptual art, and socially responsible, creative education. The project was thus carried by a highly complex fabric of relationships and interdependencies, which may have perplexed the outside viewer, yet reflects, if anything, the complexity of *real life* in our globalised world.

By networking the four European metropolises, and within the constraints of a limited time frame, the project created a panoramic view of both the cultural diversity of the participating cities and of European commonalities. Less an exchange process between different cities, it aimed to generate a joint archive – a view on self and *other* within and beyond one's own cityscape.

It is of central importance perhaps to the development of the European Union to encourage communication and comprehension between different people and societies. It is in recognition of this fact that the European Commission made 2008 the »Year of Intercultural Dialogue«. We sought to make a contribution to this aim through our project.

Thinking beyond Signs of the City

An Introduction and a Digression on Culture and European Citizenship

Uta Staiger,
European Network Co-ordinator, urban dialogues, London

As the first part of this book vividly illustrates, Signs of the City addressed a rather wide range of subjects. These, in turn, proved relevant to a number of academic disciplines and areas of research. Centrally concerned with the role of visual arts and new media in participative learning experiences, the project examined and developed methodologies from the field of youth education. Given its interest in how the participants communicated with each other using virtual and visual tools, it also, however, raised questions pertaining to cultural and media studies, as well as media pedagogy. A third emphasis was on the way in which individuals and communities perceive, use, and respond to the familiar and unfamiliar cityscapes that surround their lives; research from the fields of urban and community studies, as well as visual sociology, is highly interested in that. Finally, a dimension of Signs of the City was also relevant to European studies, as it investigated how the city becomes, as an early description had it, »a workshop for European identities« forging a particular kind of civil societal network between cultural institutions, NGOs, and universities.

These academic interests may not have been immediately present to all participants and organisers in the day-to-day running of the project, however, they informed both the underlying concept and the key elements of its delivery. One of these was an evaluation carried out by the Centre for Urban and Community Research at Goldsmiths College, which was conceived as an integral part of the project. Chapter 6 is dedicated exclusively to the set-up and outcome of this study. The other was a series of conferences held in Berlin at the House of World Cultures, and in Sofia and London in cooperation with the local Goethe Institutes, in Autumn 2008. There, academics as well as artists and practitioners, elaborated cross-disciplinarily on particular subjects, which the project had implicitly

or explicitly raised. They examined topics such as local citizenship and global networking, the role of arts organisations in participative youth education, photographic practise and identity development, or new technologies and spatial mapping. In this sense, Signs of the City also looked into different ways of knowledge production; it became a nucleus attracting and sparking research in different areas of expertise.

The intention of the following chapter is to grant an insight into some of this work by selecting four such contributions. Michael Keith, former Head of the CUCR, reads the twenty-first century city as a relational one, in which constructions of political imaginaries play out and in which visual practises and arts projects may create new urban geographies. Kristin Veel from Copenhagen University takes recourse to neuroscientific research in order to examine visual information processes in urban and digital environments. Franz-Joseph Röll from the University of Applied Science in Darmstadt turns his attention to media pedagogy and the role of intercultural communication in educational media projects. And Andrew McIlroy, a European policy advisor and author who accompanied the Berlin conference, reflects on the topics raised by Signs of the City around a number of conceptual clusters.

In complement to these rich insights, the remainder of this introduction will take a brief look at another concern that underwrote the project: the creative engagement of young people with the idea of *Europe*. If the project sought to generate knowledge on a number of topics to which it stood in close relation, one is arguably the conundrum of European citizenship: the challenges and potentials that are currently posited by it and the role culture may play in its coming into being.

Why use the term citizenship in this context? To begin with, citizenship is a key category in modern politics, which empirically describes who belongs to a political community and what rights and obligations this legal status implies. However, citizenship is also about identity, in that it articulates what it means or should mean to be a member of a political community, how solidarity and commonality may be defined, and how cultural difference can be recognised within it. Thirdly, citizenship refers to participation in public debate and decision-making; it describes the vocation that every »citizen [may play] a full and active part in the affairs of the community.« As a status, exercise, and normative ideal, citizenship is thus one possible prism through which to examine the symbols and practises of belonging, the communication of and across difference, the exploration of one's own neighbourhood and community in relation to others, and questions of access and participation – issues, which were all in one way or another central to Signs of the City.

This also already throws some light onto the role that culture may play for citizenship. On one level, *culture* is said to contribute to a feeling of belonging and identity; a shared experience through which »we make and inhabit meaningful worlds.« It is often described as an integral dimension of social life that anchors the individual and defines collectivity. While not uncontroversial, this view of culture is also about the dialogic encounter between self and other, suggesting that recognition of (cultural) difference is important for the way we live in society as equals. Not surprisingly, many of the visual explorations that the young participants of Signs of the City undertook of their closest environment were cast in these terms. They may have shown multiple, or interlocked forms of identification; however, whether group-based, urban, national, or indeed European, the *siting* of the self and engagement with the others was one element of many of their practises.

Yet there is another dimension to culture that is perhaps equally relevant to citizenship. As something people fiercely discuss, dissect, support, and oppose, it can be a vehicle for public debate which, as Jürgen Habermas put it, is key to democratic processes. Cultural activity may make particularly young people aware of and interested in sensitive topics, and provide them with creative ways to express and address not only similar but also opposing views. Incidentally, this often happens in *affective ways*. We may be rational people, but sometimes we do not reason reasonably, we argue emotionally. Affect however is arguably not detrimental, but rather complementary to rational discussion; we also make decisions on right and wrong emotionally. Emotions are »part and parcel of the system of ethical reasoning.« In other words, affect engages us; it allows emotional identification with and acting on behalf of others and thus provides a basis for an active kind of citizenship.

In both of these senses, visual practises might be more important to making us feel like citizens than we may think. In conveying social knowledge, forming collective memory, and allowing for ideology but also dissent, visual practices often harness identification and affective argument. They provide, »resources for thought and feeling that are not registered in the norms of literate rationality that constitute the discourse of political legitimacy in Western societies.« Indeed, in their visually expressed thoughts and feelings about themselves and their cities, the young participants (organisers, artists, and institutions) of Signs of the City actively and critically engaged with their urban, social, and political realities. At the same time, they also became aware of those of their peers in the other cities. This might also have personally brought up an issue for them that would previously at most have been, an abstract term: Europe.

Europe has been a big idea carried forward in very small steps; a grand ideal built on matter-of-fact and perhaps prosaic grounds. However, citizens remain to be convinced that Europe is an opportunity to shape the way we live together, interact, and engage with *our others*. While citizenship has historically been defined by a variety of institutions, from the Greek *polis* (the origins of citizenship are urban!), the Roman Empire, or since the late eighteenth century, the nation state, European integration (and since 1992, EU citizenship) raised unprecedented questions on political membership. Like the nation-state, the European Union may give us rights, but we have no obligations to it. We may technically belong to it, but do we *feel* we do? Do we know who we are in this case? Do *we* participate in its construction and discuss its decision-making? And if we don't, how legitimate is the Union as a construct?

Aware of these pressing questions, the EU interestingly enough increasingly seeks to win over its citizens with recourse to culture. It is cultural cooperation and exchange that is called upon to help to make, »European citizenship a tangible reality by encouraging direct participation by European citizens in the integration process.« Probably less than the awareness of, »their common values, history and culture as key elements of their membership of a society,« it is the curiosity and debates, the small, contested, and often empirically unverifiable steps involved in making a European project happen, that may allow something like the kernel of citizenship beyond the nation to emerge. Whether Signs of the City has contributed its small share to this remains to be seen. In any case, as the following articles show, the project also raised a whole lot of other questions, that may have been more directly pertinent for the young participants and coordinators alike. Signs of the City as a visual youth art project, with all its multiple associations, opportunities, negotiations and failings, may nevertheless have put *Europe* on the map for its participants – for some of them perhaps for the first time.

Going Europe

Rudolf Netzelmann,
Overall Project Co-ordinator, urban dialogues, Berlin

The Berlin youth art project *Archive of Signs − Inventory of a City*, carried out in 2003 by urban dialogues, was in many ways a model for the Signs of the City project and the starting point of a journey to three other European cities.

Involving unemployed young people as well as trained artists, the project took its point of departure from a straightforward but nonetheless challenging task: to photographically explore both tangible and hidden elements of and within their own urban environments. Participants literally *captured* urban signs, discussed their form and possible significance with other members of their teams, and thereby created an archive of signs and images of their own cities.

This work was participative, as the artists operated as facilitators and moderators rather than as educators. They supported the young photographers, helped them to refine their photographic techniques, and worked with them to present and exhibit their work effectively. Such project work proved to be interesting not only because it led to unusual outcomes, but also because it helped participants to express, playfully and courageously, their own ways of seeing and perceiving. It also provided the facilitators with a chance to combine artistic with media-pedagogical methods; the participating young people gained access to an art form, from which they had up to then felt far removed. At the same time, it seemed that both the content and the methods employed by this pilot project might lend themselves to exportation − could this idea be tested elsewhere in Europe? The answer to this question came in the form of the Signs of the City project. In the following, I will take a closer look at some of the stages, resources, and impressions that can be gleaned from its journey across, and to, Europe.

Every city is a palimpsest. Urban signs can tell us about the past, about other generations, other cultures, and their legacies. The local present is intimately linked with (European) history and biographies. The signs of today's city also evoke the personal memories of its residents; memories, which invite us to compare and indeed understand our own background within a constantly changing urban scenario. Making our way through the city, through its urban, architectural, and social spaces, we continuously find ourselves in both familiar and unfamiliar terrain. The correspondence, which we might discover between the away and intimate spaces, can itself be captured in images: it can be compared and articulated visually as well as verbally.

Big cities are nodal points, in which creation, transformation and destruction permanently take place. Cultures meet, mix and separate. Cities rely on representation and constantly seek to communicate themselves through images and signs. Thus, they also challenge our capacity to perceive and process such a visual overload.

If it were possible to use the city of Berlin as a resource for our geographical, historical, and biographical rootedness, as we explored in the pilot project described above, why shouldn't it also be possible elsewhere? We are the heirs of *Europe*, after all, its citizens and if anything the builders of its future. What if we leave our familiar terrain, if we look further than the end of our noses to explore other European cities, to see and understand them with the help of the digital camera? This would also be a journey and a method, which (based on our experience, at least) is closer to artists than to teachers or tourist guides, and which they could undertake with trained or even unqualified young people. *Travel educates*: it seemed plausible that with and through the exploration of other cities, the participants' perspectives on their own homes and selves could well be enriched. The focus for such a venture had already been found in the Berlin pilot: the Signs of the City.

BERLIN, BARCELONA, LONDON, SOFIA

The journey took us to London, Sofia, and Barcelona. There, we were able to involve artists, institutions, organisations, and networks in the project. These cities were of particular interest to us, as they stood for both cultural density and intercultural diversity. Social, economic, and political upheavals certainly leave traces in popular memory, but they also leave them in today's signs and urban landscapes.

INITIAL DRIVE

The journey *towards* Europe was only feasible with further resources. The project initiators succeeded in convincing three key institutions, among others, of the potentials of Signs of the City.

The EU-Programme Culture 2007-2013 funds this kind of project as long as it complies with their own programme objectives and has the capacity to generate added value beyond the duration and the direct participants of the project proper. Similarly, the German Capital Cultural Fund supports projects that are culturally innovative, hold a significant potential for the German capital, and have the capacity to make an impact nationally and internationally. The German Goethe Institute in Bulgaria found the project proposal a persuasive contribution to German-Bulgarian intercultural dialogue within a European framework; its contribution as a project partner made the Bulgarian part of the project practicable.

Essentially, the EU Culture Programme seeks to support initiatives that foster both respect for and appreciation of cultural heterogeneity within Europe. This objective, of course, rests on a rather uncomfortable insight: the programmes are there to address the fact that diversity often challenges and strains communities; ultimately, it often leads either to the aggressive rejection of the cultural *other*, or to the superficial appropriation of the *other* that lacks recognition and respect.

The EU hopes for and supports projects that make culture and art not only accessible to particular social groups, but to virtually everyone. It seeks to promote social and civil societal integration through such projects.

The EU respects the importance of art and culture for education. There now exist numerous projects and studies, that prove that artists and artistic methods add new approaches to the educational domain. As EU experts testify, such approaches may encourage students to become more active and curious. Creative methods can increase their interest in learning: they are found to be more sensitive, concrete, and effective than traditional forms of education.

The EU wishes for a dialogue of cultures and an exchange of artists across Europe; it promotes the creation of new networks in the arts and cultural sectors, and cooperation between producers of culture.

PROJECT WORK – INTERCULTURAL AND INTERDISCIPLINARY

The Signs project proposal was selected for financial support from Brussels, because it attended to many of the above mentioned objectives. On this basis, additional resources from other funding bodies could be mobilised. After several years of preparation, we also saw a network of partners emerge that was prepared to plan and deliver a series of activities, including workshops, conferences, exhibitions, and meetings. Many virtual and real encounters took place between and across the four participating cities, supported and sustained by partner organisations with expertise in youth art, media, pedagogy, and community work. Just like the project itself, the range of working approaches proved highly diverse, and often informed by local or national sociocultural traditions and by participatory approaches. While the emphasis in Barcelona was on community work, the London workshops focussed on media art, and in Sofia social-psychological methods for working in »transitory spaces« were developed (cf. Winnicott). The concept of Signs of the City deliberately left room for all the actors involved to develop their own approaches and functions within the project.

In this sense, the project also aimed to stimulate an intercultural dialogue about both the project process and its desired outcomes. The working conditions and ways of recruiting were also adjusted to respective local conditions. In Sofia, the young participants were recruited through online social networking sites, while in Barcelona the workshops drew on the constituencies of their local social and community centres. In London, the project managers contacted arts organisations or drop-in centres, and in Berlin, workshops were organised in collaboration with skills-based vocational training centres. This range of working conditions in a sense provided a laboratory for arts and education programmes; it demonstrates just how diverse the conditions and opportunities for cultural, social, and artistic work are across Europe.

Needless to say, such methodological diversity also poses considerable challenges in terms of project management: to synchronise and transfer activities, or to compare outcomes, is a daunting task. Certainly, one of the most significant challenges was to distribute and assess available resources in each partner city, and to understand the working cycles they could thus fund. In Berlin, for instance, the six month-long vocational training courses were financed by job centres, thus allowing for long-term, practise-oriented, participative, and conceptually varied engagement with higher learning prospects. Here, the artists had more freedom and time to guide individual participants than in cities where such work could only take place in blocks of a few days at a time, or in weekly cycles. Nevertheless, the effect of such condensed project work on individual participants should not be underestimated.

Just as the original idea for the project came out of a very specific local setting, its transference to other places could only be successful by taking the destination's local needs and conditions fully into account. The project partners took on this task of *translation*; a challenge that often exposed the limits of what is feasible in a collaborative project such as this. This publication seeks to document how this challenge was nonetheless met in the course of the project and to illustrate – desired as well as unexpected – the outcomes it produced. Particularly chapter 1, presenting the methods and concepts of selected workshops, and chapter 6, written by Dr. Alison Rooke from the Centre for Urban and Community Research, will grant an insight into this. Indeed, the project initiators had approached CUCR staff at the very beginning of the preparatory phase in order to ensure that the project would be evaluated and accompanied academically. With this, they hoped to gain greater insight into the process and the outcomes of a project such as this, and thus also to contribute to best practise.

Belonging, Intercultural Dialogues

How can the visualisation of urban landscapes stimulate a feeling, a sense of belonging and a sense of the city's (cultural) spaces? In the Signs of the City project this question was explored on two levels. First, virtually, the online image archive linked the four project sites and thus allowed young participants from one city to explore the urban photographs of their peers in the other three. Second, physically, the LAB 2 exchange programme provided the chance for some of the young photographers to meet in a real direct encounter, visit one of the

cities in person, and jointly explore it with their peers (cf. Chapter 2), mapping and discovering familiar and unfamiliar cityscapes photographically. Both activities sought to instigate dialogue on selfhood and alterity. This was the project's very own way of encouraging the, »recognition of and respect for the heterogeneity of cultures,« which is so poignantly expressed in the EU's Culture 2007 programme. This meant that all participants had to negotiate and dissect prevalent clichés and stereotypes; to rethink and rearticulate personal impressions in the workshops. They walked through the cities individually or in groups, *experienced* their trajectories and *digested* the perceived impressions photographically. To take pictures in a foreign country – of a house, an unknown symbol, or a traffic sign commented upon with graffiti – can mean that we emotionally engage with, perhaps appropriate, but also certainly recognise an unfamiliar cultural space.

To talk about these images, indeed to compare them with similar ones from home, can heighten our awareness of the differences, but also the similarities between these cultural spaces. Evidently, there are structural differences between experiencing an encounter in another city or country and observing it online; yet they do not necessarily have to be mutually exclusive. What matters however is that the act of taking photographs also served to generate and exchange signs, which in turn sparked conversations – spontaneously, following an apparently omnipresent (or intercultural?) impulse.

The organisations and artists involved in LAB 2 worked more as facilitators than as educators. One interesting conclusion from this is that an image may represent and reveal something of the photographer that cannot as such be put into words – least of all the words of a foreign language. An image anchors conversations and at the same encourages them to open up to others. In this sense, perhaps, Signs of the City may have achieved a very particular kind of intercultural dialogue: one that opened up new cultural spaces to the participants. The photographic capture may have signalled the beginning of a social and civil societal recognition of the other.

Signs

The project did not issue binding guidelines to its partners regarding the *reading* of the city. Nonetheless, and without any academicism, all workshops approached these signs similarly. Signs were seen as carriers of meanings, which point to something else, which seek an addressee, and which invite a response from photographers. Indeed, the project sparked a whole host of archaeological, ethnological, and criminological curiosities. It is interesting, in this context, to what extent the project also revealed a seemingly cross-cultural if latent consensus *not* to take signs at their face value: to mistrust the manifold visual surfaces of the city and to be indifferent to the touristic enhanced icons and *guidance* (i.e., traffic) signs. Could we speak of an intercultural consensus, which already assumes that meaning is hidden away, that the city dweller needs to unearth and construct meaning out of a kaleidoscope of disjointed segments? The artists generally distinguished between prefabricated and found signs and those created by the photographer him or herself. Generally, however, it proved particularly productive to have the young photographers develop their own feel for things, and pick and choose from the urban jigsaw puzzle what most interested them. In any case, of course, these signs were always about two meanings at the same time – the meaning a sign may have for the beholder and the (apparent) meaning it has within the urban environment. Given that signs – standardised traffic signage, pictogrammes, logos, advertising, but also informal street-art signs – only reveal their meaning with reference to what they are there to represent, they are good vehicles with which to encourage communication. Only in conversation with insiders or by researching the background of signs may we really grasp their significance. This interplay between image and *word*, between photographic capture and discussions within the team, became the project's core methodology.

THE MAGIC AND POWER OF IMAGES

The Signs of the City project produced numerous images – and images of images – of urban space. The city was *read* as itself pictorial, as an entity literally created in order to make an impact on the observer *qua* image (that is, as a tourist icon, an architectonic arrangement, or an urban scenario). Images, and not only personal ones, are fascinating; they can seduce, they activate emotions and can become virtually animated. Unlike signs, images practically look at the observer and put a spell on him or her. This quasi-mysterious property is both typical of images and independent of the objects they represent. It provided rich material for all of the workshops. To produce images/ photographs perhaps gives us a sense of power to arrange the world according to our own wishes. Perhaps the photographs evoke images of us and of our desires, which are seemingly hidden in their reflection, and thus come curiously alive. They may make the observer emotionally self-aware. Often, media projects are said to exert a peculiar kind of magnetism on the actors, which is independent of their specific object and which may rather have to do with this performative bringing-into-play of our own personality. The dynamics and the engagement

of the young people with visual media, which was apparent throughout the workshops, perhaps give further proof of this observation.

The creation of images, whether as a process of perception and design or as a technical practice, was often itself the object of discussion during the workshops. This, in fact, often resulted in a sobering kind of cross-current: the everyday and virtually automatic form of seeing (cf. Kristin Veel in chapter 5) was dismantled; group discussions closely analysed the way we perceive and the way images operate. If this led at times to a visual *disenchantment*, it also often meant that the participants gained significantly in terms of their visual competence.

Images and signs are charged with messages and suggestions. They can easily be used to induce a certain kind of behaviour, be it in the name of social order or commercial consumption. Of the two, it is in fact more difficult to control the effect of images than of signs (cf. H. Belting). The surfaces of today's big cities in general use both genres, which of course raises serious questions regarding the power that the producers of such hybrid image-signs have over the awareness and the behaviour of their addressees. Such production of images is, needless to say, global and develops in rather straightforward patterns. Perhaps the workshops managed to make the participants but also the artists rethink and rearticulate this particular, often automatic and unnoticed power, that comes with both images and signs.

▸ LONDON

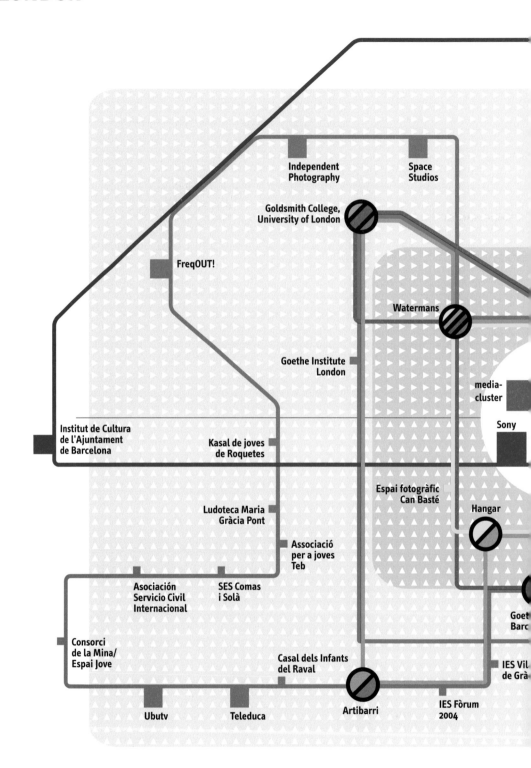

Independent
Photography

Space
Studios

Goldsmith College,
University of London

FreqOUT!

Watermans

Goethe Institute
London

media-
cluster

Sony

Institut de Cultura
de l'Ajuntament
de Barcelona

Kasal de joves
de Roquetes

Espai fotogràfic
Can Basté

Hangar

Ludoteca Maria
Gràcia Pont

Associació
per a joves
Teb

Asociación
Servicio Civil
Internacional

SES Comas
i Solà

Goet
Barc

Consorci
de la Mina/
Espai Jove

Casal dels Infants
del Raval

IES Vil
de Grà

Ubutv

Teleduca

Artibarri

IES Fòrum
2004

▴ BARCELONA

Network Map

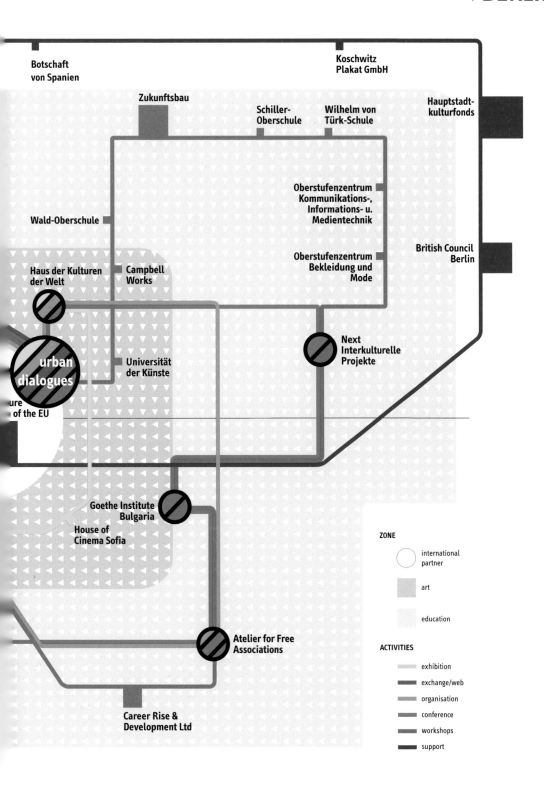

BERLIN

Botschaft von Spanien

Koschwitz Plakat GmbH

Zukunftsbau

Schiller-Oberschule

Wilhelm von Türk-Schule

Hauptstadt-kulturfonds

Oberstufenzentrum Kommunikations-, Informations- u. Medientechnik

Wald-Oberschule

British Council Berlin

Haus der Kulturen der Welt

Campbell Works

Oberstufenzentrum Bekleidung und Mode

Next Interkulturelle Projekte

urban dialogues

Universität der Künste

ure of the EU

Goethe Institute Bulgaria

House of Cinema Sofia

Atelier for Free Associations

Career Rise & Development Ltd

ZONE

○ international partner

art

education

ACTIVITIES

exhibition
exchange/web
organisation
conference
workshops
support

SOFIA

Workshops

chapter one

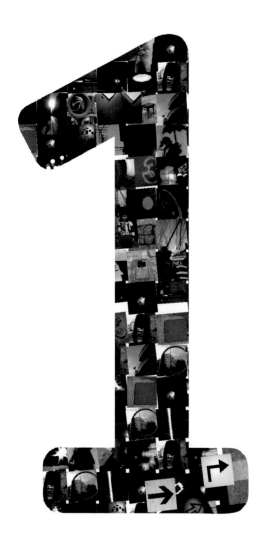

The Workshops: Introduction

Britt Hatzius,
Artists Network Co-ordinator, urban dialogues, London

Thirty-four workshops led by thirty artists with around 330 young people took place over a period of one year in the four participating cities: Berlin, London, Barcelona and Sofia. Spanning a wide range of artistic and methodological approaches, the workshops embraced locally specific sociocultural conditions and realities. Participants came from different social, cultural and educational backgrounds, embarking on a photographic exploration that would enable them to express their own views and perspectives on their urban environments. The artists were not only facilitators of these explorations; they were crucial conversation partners, accompanying the young people's work and supporting them with ideas, inspiration, and advice where needed. The organisations, institutions, community centres and schools played just as important a part in providing a creative working environment as the work developed within the workshops themselves.

The image server »citipix« was specifically created for this project and became the first meeting point of all photographs uploaded in the four different cities. It functioned as a trigger for conversations within different workshop groups; comparing photographs taken by one individual with those taken by another, photographs taken in one city with those taken in another. The information included with each of the uploaded images, such as keywords, categories, and emotional ratings chosen by the photographer, adds a rich and detailed inventory and an additional dimension to the collection of photographs. This intensive uploading process of analysing and naming each image slowed down the otherwise familiar web 2.0 photo-uploading procedure and allowed for more in-depth verbal communication about the images and their possible meanings. It was in these workshops that personal working processes, explorations, discussions and presentations all came together to form the basis of the project.

PROCESS AND OUTCOME

Looking through the thousands of photographs on the »citipix« website can at times seem, overwhelming. Creating series, stripes and visual choreographies helps to make sense of the photographs we flick through. The time spent on one or the other photograph will probably determine how much detail is discovered and how much we know or want to know about the person who has chosen to capture that particular frame.

The photographs themselves are all signs of young people's engagement; visual engagement with their urban environment. It was not only about the moment of capturing the images; it also involved the dialogue and translation that went on before, during and after. This underlying process might easily be overlooked when faced with the mass of resulting photographs. It is precisely this process of engagement though that lies at the heart of the Signs of the City project. Guided by artists with a range of different backgrounds, skills and visions of what this process might be, groups of young people were encouraged to explore their environments by focusing, recognising and extracting details from the surrounding sea of visual encounters.

CONCEPTS AND IDEAS

The various types of frameworks within which the young photographers were able to articulate their own perspectives using visual, verbal, or gestural means were developed by thirty different artists. To provide an initial starting point, an inspiration, an idea, or a concept for the young photographers meant to open up familiar grounds to new ways of seeing. From a pinhole camera to a mobile phone, from literal signs and symbols to physical interventions with space and questions of identity, each workshop had its own very distinctive approach and process. Using a medium as accessible as photography is today, the artistic frameworks proposed by the artists were invaluable in reflecting not only on the medium itself but in giving the young participants an opportunity to focus and select, providing tools to create meaningful connections.

JOURNEYS AND DISCOVERIES

The selection of workshops presented here will highlight the very different approaches with which the artists chose to work with their groups of young people. Some of these workshops show young photographers investigating particular themes or concepts suggested by the artist, while others show how simple starting points can open up an unpredictable array of interpretations, where the artist is guided by the young photographers, as much as they might be guided by the artist. This process of negotiation, exploration, and collaboration between artist and young photographer is an important step in exposing some of the more complex and invisible ways of communicating views. These different frameworks allowed each workshop to take on its own individual character and significance. Highly-developed artistic input, diversity in the interpretation of »signs« and openness towards various different ways of working enabled Signs of the City to become more than simply an educational endeavour or a collection of photographs. Each workshop

was able to take on its own momentum, creating its own discursive environment and local relevance while remaining embedded within a larger network. The goal was not to solely accumulate visual imagery, but to embark on a journey from initial ideas, to photographic exposures, to a reflective discursiveness, and through to uploading images online.

These journeys are described in the following eight workshops as examples of how different ways of working can allow for young people's critical and reflective engagement with the constantly changing urban environments of these four different cities.

SIMILARITIES AND DIFFERENCES

At the Arts and Education Lab in autumn 2007, when all the artists came together to discuss ideas and approaches for their own workshops, the disparateness of working methods and understandings of what it means to work with young people was acknowledged as a crucial way of allowing differences to emerge and unfold. The basic structure and intention was clear, but nothing was prescribed. The leeway that was left for ways in which Signs of the City could be interpreted was risky, with respect to its coherence, but eye-opening in its ability to draw out an unexpected wealth of ideas and approaches. The workshops were seen as opportunities to share different points of views, be it between one young photographer and another, between them and the artist, or between a group in one city and another. It is this diversity, as well as a space for both differences and similarities that we hope to present with this selection of workshops.

Campbell Works

Neil Taylor and Harriet Murray work with students
of Wilhelm-von-Türk-School in Potsdam

London-based artists Neil Taylor and Harriet Murray, labelling as Campbell Works, worked with fifteen pupils from the Wilhelm-von-Türk-School in Potsdam. The school is specially equipped for students with hearing impairments. In Campbell Works' own words, »We can follow the project from its first ideas to the learning experience of artists and students alike throughout.«

We were invited to take part in the Berlin cluster of Signs of the City. The project kicked off at the Arts and Education Lab in autumn 2007 at the House of World Cultures (HKW) in Berlin. It was an exciting three days with a packed programme of presentations, open debate, speed dating, and intellectual duelling. The emphasis was for all participating artists, technicians, directors, and facilitators to meet and to get to know each other through developing key issues involved within the project. Many hours were spent discussing different aspects of the project from ethical and international legal issues to its technical implementation. We collectively explored the function of the public website and its usability for the Signs of the City photographers.

We were given the opportunity to determine our own framework for delivery and through the A&E lab we developed the embryo of an idea. By exploring the inherent core values within the project that lay beyond the pictorial surface of the website, we asked what was at its inner heart that excited us? We wished to find meaning beyond practical engagement and to work out an approach that would satisfy all involved. There clearly needed to be a definite outcome – photos for the website – and we desired a meaningful and exciting exchange between both the participants and ourselves. Through the A&E lab we began to identify an opening. Assuming that one of the aims of Signs of the City was to take a snapshot of city life seen through the eyes of Europe's youth, then as many different representatives should be included as possible. The range of participating countries was as good as the finance would allow and the groups seemed fairly diverse in their catchments. But none included young people with a recognised disability.

We discussed the possibility of including deaf participants, intrigued by the idea of working with a group that may potentially have a very different relationship and experience of »city« than ourselves.

The unknown excited us, as we had no prior experience of this particular disability. Following on from research undertaken for a previous Campbell Works project titled MindMine, created in 2006, we wished to explore how perceptions can vary for the hearing impaired, and which if any of the other senses are enhanced to take on the role of the missing sensory input. Hearing is part of our communication system but so is sight; so, do deaf people see the world differently? And what in the urban landscape attracts their attention? Do they see details and notice more incidental moments that are missed as a result of the audio clutter of our cities?

WORKSHOP

Our approach was to try to examine some fundamentals of communication, to explore the possibility of communicating largely through pictures and actions and not a recognised language; to learn how this section of society views its environment and what happens when their normal communication preferences are not understood. Could we with our minimal grasp of both German and sign language make ourselves understood and make it a meaningful experience for the participants? Whatever the outcome, it made for an interesting scenario. Having met a few of the students we were feeling relatively confident, as they were very quick on the uptake and eager to engage in the project. The success of the workshops would hinge largely on the enthusiastic support of Gisela and Birgit, who worked alongside as signing and German translators.

The focus of the project being on photography, we were interested in creating an approach that would allow the participants a rewind from digital technologies back to the birth of photography, the aim being to inform their thinking by creating a dialogue between the photographer and the instrument of image capture. In order to retain mobility we developed a portable darkroom that could be transported and erected almost anywhere, and used it to develop large format black and white images in the »field.«

On arrival we were greeted by the fifteen dynamic and enthusiastic participants, eager to start their photographic odyssey. Using fundamental analogue principles, the photographers constructed large format pinhole cameras from found cardboard boxes, quickly learning of the need to tape all the joints in order to block out the light. With a digital camera in one hand and their pinhole camera in the other they set out to explore their surroundings. As they began returning to the darkroom »base camp« they learned how to develop and fix their images. Examining their results, they assessed the pros and cons of 150 years of technological advancement as they struggled with long exposure times and cardboard camera shake.

It quickly became apparent that their focus was largely on portraiture, photographing each other within familiar surroundings. This was a rather unexpected result as the project brief was »to explore their urban landscape« and we had collectively discussed ways of seeing and what material might make interesting pictures. We realised that for them and perhaps all teenagers the most immediate and interesting subjects are friends.

The weather was not good and forced exposure times of up to 90 seconds, requiring subjects to stand still; this was immediately identified by several participants as an opportunity for new imagery. The combination of these factors and the wind blowing the lightweight cameras created ethereal imagery with »ghosts« barely visible within the landscape. Some students became fascinated by this process and started to explore the possibilities it offered.

In the glowing red darkness of the developing tent, the pinhole negatives were transformed into positive composite images. The students began to overlay cut paper stencils onto their negatives and immediately created new signage and narratives. Several students had already discovered the invert function on the digital cameras, allowing immediate viewing of their pinhole image. We were also able to create a wonderful juxtaposition of technologies by attaching a GPS device to the cardboard cameras to log and map the »globally positioned situations« of the pinhole exposures.

Already so fluent with digital immediacy, not all participants saw many benefits of this physical and cumbersome analogue approach. To walk around the city or stand in a public space next to a strange cardboard box and not feel self-conscious is hard. You have to be keen or oblivious not to be mildly embarrassed, and, as a group of young people who do not generally want to draw attention to themselves, there were issues for some about the spectacle of a long exposure and being seen carrying the cardboard cameras.

Overall there was a buzz and excited anticipation about the project as images emerged from the darkness of the tent, with many extraordinary pictures created. The participants made huge strides in image making, seeing the potential to use their negatives and stencil making to create wholly new works, and compositional arrangements.

Towards the end of the workshop we collectively discussed the work and encouraged the selection of images, both digital and pinhole, that would be uploaded to the website. We digitally converted the pinhole selection and bravely approached the school's computer suite. With the calm dedication of one of the photographers and a little bit of system excavation we overcame all technical difficulties and they were off, uploading at the pace of a speedy snail. While waiting for each picture to be accepted, the students got busy populating their own networking sites with their images and getting instant feedback from other deaf users.

The upload process went relatively smoothly, however, an unforeseen problem arose with the need to tag images for the database search functions. The complexity of tagging images

REFLEXION

The participating photographers were as mixed in their creative interests and skills as any group of fifteen teenagers. But, the emotional perceptions and speed at which the students gathered information from their surroundings seemed significantly faster than those of us who rely on our ears, and their ability to assimilate learning was impressive.

Many of our projects involve the creation of disorientating environments, and during these workshops the students' reliance on their visual communication systems was severely hampered when they worked within the darkroom tent. This loss of communication systems, both verbal and visual, strangely created an atmosphere of calm, a kind of »lost at sea« feeling for all involved. As artists, we were working within an »alien« communicative environment and now the participants were experiencing it, too. By removing the ability to communicate through conventional channels, they were forced to learn from each other's actions and encouraged to take risks even if it meant making mistakes. The framework allowed for the creation of new imagery within an experimental platform by dissolving the conversational communication systems, including signing. Herein, practical activity became the form of communication. The imagery that the photographers produced is beautiful, compelling, and ethereal, and their upload selection will remain as a legacy to the project; it easily speaks for itself. However, we hope that a deeper legacy has been left in the students' ability to question, learn from, and act on their actions and imaginations, as they did during the five days in which we had the pleasure of being with them.

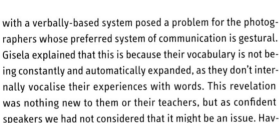

with a verbally-based system posed a problem for the photographers whose preferred system of communication is gestural. Gisela explained that this is because their vocabulary is not being constantly and automatically expanded, as they don't internally vocalise their experiences with words. This revelation was nothing new to them or their teachers, but as confident speakers we had not considered that it might be an issue. Having identified this, we were soon able to explore details within their pictures that they could create tags for and discuss what kind of words they might use.

This experience exposed a recurring theme of translation and communication that seemed to run through both our workshop and the wider framework for Signs of the City. One of the aims for the website was that it be infinitely searchable by picture narrative, creating new collections of photos with each search, but the very mechanism needed to create this picture-based collage is a linguistic system susceptible to translation interpretations.

The Barcelona Experience

Javier Rodrigo, ArtiBarri Network

Artibarri is a network that advocates art for social change based on citizen participation and community work. Its name is an amalgam of the Catalan words for »art« and »neighbourhood«. Artibarri collaborated with a number of other community arts organisations in Barcelona to produce the workshops and the exhibition. The collaborators include Hangar.org, Teleduca, Associació per a joves Teb, Kasal de joves de Roquetes, Consorci de la Mina / Espai Jove, and Ubu TV. These groups were able to conduct the workshops in a variety of Barcelona's neighbourhoods: Ciutat Vella, Sans, Poble Nou, Nou barris, La Barceloneta, Raval, La Mina, and Poble Sec.

Ten workshops were conducted in Barcelona, led by the artists: Mapi Aramendia, Núria Calafell, Pamela Gallo, Paula Kleiman, Andréas Lang, Núria Marquès, Javier Oliden, Javier Rodrigo, and Almendra Salazar.

Aiming to change young people's perspectives, the workshops mostly explored urban spaces in their closest surroundings or took trips to other districts to discover the different signs of the city. Various topics came up in the process of selecting and editing images, through collective street action and dynamic group debates, and in processes of teaching visual literacy through the language of photography.

WORKSHOPS

The teams belonging to each workshop were extremely diverse; on the one hand the nature of each group participating in the project differed while on the other hand, each of them explored very different neighbourhoods of the city. Groups of young people from youth centres, of different culture, and origins who were aged between fourteen and eighteen [Teb, Roquetas, Ubu TV with the Casal dels Infants del Raval o la Mina (the Raval and Mina House of Children)] formed one end of the spectrum. The other was formed by working groups of »older« people aged between twenty and thirty (the Ubu TV workshop), student groups supported by their school (Teleduca in Trinitat Vella), Catalan student groups who participated in their free time (Gràcia), and informal working groups (Teleduca Sans).

All of the workshops embodied collaborative working spaces in which the artists were able to work hand in hand with educational trainers, and in which they themselves had the opportunity to relate intensely to both the educational work and the performance context. For example, in two of the Teleduca workshops, one of the teachers of the two cooperating institutes always supervised the process. Ubu TV followed the same pattern during the development of the school programmes, working directly with social educators from the Raval Children's

Centre (Casal de Infants de Raval) to integrate the informal education perspective. In contrast, Roquetas, La Mina, and Teb worked with their usual team of professionals, which incorporated various artists working and designing together.

It must be emphasised that the topics chosen correspond to the strong interactive concept that is fundamental to the core of Signs of the City; debates always evolved about the topics and the types of signs that the groups wished to present, which was in turn always negotiated within the different groups: in Teb and Reoquetas, for example, the young people chose their own starting points. The youths from the Teleduca workshop chose topics that were of interest to them from a photographic view; they worked with various concepts of photographic language, acted like a tourists in their own neighbourhood, looked for their own identities within the city, or even focussed on more formal aspects. To give another example, the La Mina workshop attempted to show that spaces belong to their own identities and that their relationships must to be grasped in a closer way. The approach taken by Ubu TV was to make various trips and excursions while persisting in debating the editing and selection of topics.

All of this exploratory work was expressed in different types of series or pictures in which each youth or each team worked to highlight significant topics of their interest; they revealed such diverse signs and topics as migration, physical borders of the metropolis, and the identities of these youths (Trinitat Vella), incorporating their very own places (Teb), spaces of social interaction, and signs which represent other cultures (Teleduca Sans) including popular culture and the legacy of the gypsies (La Mina). Signs and topics also dealt with urban and social landscape at the marketplaces of the diverse neighbourhoods (Teb or Teleduca), with life in the squares (Teleduca in Gràcia and Sans) or life at the beach (Roquetes at daytime, and el Teb at night time), with places of meeting and communication, for example telephone booths or the leisure areas used by immigrants and different communities (Teleduca in Sans and el Teb). A final mention must be given to the workshops in which the young people dealt with diverse topics; from considering a series of pictures to realising assorted series of photos: culinary signs, money signs, poetic signs (Ubu TV with the SIC).

REFLEXION

In order to analyse the workshops, it is important to mention that the artists and educational trainers underlined the significance of working in groups throughout each phase of the project; from the starting point to managing the cameras, to passing them on, to talking to different people, and to editing and positioning the signs and different topics in unison. The artists emphasised that in the course of the various stages of the project the youths acquired »a new perspective and became more supportive«, that they »became more involved« (Teleduca, Sans); that they learned »to work together in a group and to start a trip together« (Roquetas); or that they discovered »more about themselves and about the things the city contains« (Teleduca, Trinitat Vella). Social interaction became a focal point of the field work. It evolved through the collective experience of taking pictures in the city by going out to the district of Barceloneta and its beach, by looking at life around the harbours of Barcelona, or places of great history (Ubu TV), as well as by observing the leisure time of the inhabitants of the district of Gràcia or its peculiarities as characterised by the youths from the district (Teleduca, Gràcia). Pictures were also taken of »nonyouth spaces« (Teb) through collective actions or trips and by discovering the manner in which many immigrants deal with their lives in the surroundings of Sans or the Industrial Park (parque industrial / Teleduca Sans).

All of this reflective and explorative work marked a change in the conception and perception of the city. It can be assumed that lots of the young people »appreciated their neighbourhood and the history behind it« (Gràcia) or »discovered new manners in which to look at the city and the people, thanks to having learned to stop and then look, analyse and take pictures in a different way« (Ubu TV). Therefore, they learned to take a more reflective look at the city and to adopt »a second look which helps them to see their city with different eyes« (Teleduca Sans). Furthermore, many of the pictures expressed the complex identities of the young people and the topics that they are concerned with in their daily lives and within their families (La Mina, Trinitat Vella). In contrast, some pictures showed new, surprising, and exotic spaces, which had been unknown to them before (Ubu TV or Roquetas). There were also inclusive aspects of the lives of the poor, changing the view and attitudes of the youths towards them (Sans, Teleduca). This initiated a process of questioning the different habits of the city and its residents and of analysing the differences that exist in the various districts.

For most of the artists, the challenge lay in their organisational collaboration with Artibarri to analyse and evaluate their youth work in detail. For others it was the experience of using the camera as a tool to change views and thereby work with different young people to see the world from their perspectives and neighbourhoods. The workshops were enriched by the youths' high levels of motivation and the scale of alternative forms which dealt with the city from a visual culture perspective.

In this sense, working with the signs (Gracia, Trinitat Vella or La Mina), looking at the city of Barcelona in other districts (Ubu TV or Roquetas), or analysing what it is like to see the city with different eyes (Sans) was also an opportunity to analyse the daily, self-repeating reality of young people.

Apart from the fact that lots of workshops were related to community institutions such as the Teb, Roquetas, or Teleduca, the opportunity to exchange opinions, to evaluate, and work towards a final exhibition was of great advantage and proved to be a motivating benefit. A further advantage was the collaboration with different kinds of institutions in the process of introducing practical photographic experience into youth centres as in the case of the Raval Children's Centre (Casals de Infants del Raval), the »Neighbourhood Time, Time to Share Education« programme (»Temps de Barri, temps educatiu compartit«), the Ludoteca, and the cooperation of the different institutes.

The project cooperation gave many of Barcelona's artists an opportunity to exchange practical experience, to learn of different kinds of work, and to learn about alternative forms of youth work.

Finally, the great work carried out by participants of the workshops in cooperation with HANGAR deserves a special mention. They must be credited for producing the material for the exhibition (to be more specific: the participants of the Teleduca, La Mina, and Ubu TV workshops). This initiative evolved from an initial coordination meeting with HANGAR in 2007. It was decided to bring together the interactive youth workshops in a final exhibition that would be the last great workshop of the project. This and the cooperation with HANGAR led a mixed team of educational trainers and artists to design the exhibition. The process was carried out in a series of workshops, divided into four sessions in July, where the youths could experiment with different exhibition formats as well as various communication methods and ways to present their products.

For the overall cooperation, the exhibition marked one final piece of a common learning process between the designers of the workshops on the one hand and the young people on the other. Above all, it also boosted the participation of the youths in the last presentation of their contributions: the final exhibition of Signs of the City in Can Basté, in October 2008.

Construct your own Sign

Diego Ferrari works in the House of World Cultures, Berlin

When Diego Ferrari first visited the House of World Cultures for the Arts and Education Lab in autumn 2007, he was immediately taken by this landmark modernist building. A workshop in Signs of the City should find a stage in the House and its surrounding government buildings.

»As an artist working with the medium of photography, I'm interested in the quality of immanence, in the intensity of the moment and the immediacy of our existences. The inherent relationship between the immanence of human existence and the twenty-first century city is what I explored with the photographers participating in the artist-led workshop project Signs of the City, delivered in Berlin at the House of World Cultures in May 2008.«

Ferrari believes that it has become increasingly problematic to find a free emotional and personal response to public space; problematic because of the commodification, surveillance and regulation of this space. As a result he goes to the very heart of public space in his workshop; the government district of the German capital and the congress hall, built in the 1950s as a »shining beacon of liberty« (to put it in the words of the architect). Rather than aiming to depict signs found in that part of the city, Ferrari challenged the participants to construct their own sign in the city in his workshop.

»This method provoked an emotional and personal response in participants by including in the process of photographing the notion of a multidisciplinary approach to photography; a playful process which allows for an act of artistic interconnectivity between photography, ephemeral installation, happening and public space. This transforms participants' understanding of photography, and its relationship to immanence – to the immediacy of their existences, and to where they are, at that moment, in space and time. Photography becomes not so much an activity or art form but a method of communication, an attitude of freedom and autonomy, in both the personal and the sociopolitical public realm.«

The modern city is full of commodified signs. Public space, with its original promised values of democracy, has become more and more occupied by the market and also simultaneously more and more supervised, in the name of public order and »security«. Some of this occupation is obvious and objectively visible, but other aspects are internal, hidden, and subjective. Affluence, noise, messages engineered to produce consumption – all create a significant barrier to the subjective nature of being in the city, to the individual's experience of urban environment, and, on a larger scale, to the phenomenology of self.

»I gave the photographers the task of finding their own responses to the city, of challenging social codes of authority, consumption, and the public mechanisms of daily life in the city. They were asked to come up with a personal and resolute approach that was not about establishing a line of argument or a theoretical position, but rather about being bodies in space, experiencing their values and conditions embedded in the public urban environment.«

The task was to contribute to making a visual representation through play and risk-taking; from there the photographers could each generate a practical process of how they perceived, represented, and responded to the social situations that they had created through their actions. Thus, they challenged the idea of photography, as an experience that explored notions of freedom and autonomy in both the personal and public realms rather than a technical representation intended to depict reality. This proved to be a challenging in retrospective, an ultimately rewarding approach to photography for the participating photographers.

»The idea of these workshops was to instigate an act of freedom within the regulated social built environment, and thus to explore notions of freedom and autonomy in both the personal and sociopolitical realms.«

THE WORKSHOP

»In my workshops we recognised the instant quality of digital photography, and of the entire Signs of the City project, which is posted on the web. However, we concentrated on slowing down time, rather than grasping the instant, on taking a decisive action that evolved from both the act of depicting a subject and *capturing* an intuitive or rational process that constructed the concept of the image. In this way, as Vilem Flusser writes, ›In the act of photography the camera does the will of the photographers but the photographer has to will what the camera can do‹«.

The participants were challenged to move in space, patrolling their own boundaries, to be cognisant of their creativity as a potential tool to build social skills and relations. The speed at which they had to grasp the urban territory and their fluidity in formulating a response, using not only photography but also installation or performance art, made them acutely aware of how artistic and social values are intertwined.

FREEDOM AND REGULATION

»I asked the participants to respond to the challenges presented by the public space – of speed, of regulations, of the presence of the public – with naturalness and instinct, but also to take a conceptual approach. As soon as we think of representing an emotion, we naturally express it not as a single thought or frozen image; we mostly tend to express a series of events, as we would write a literary narrative or observe in a film. The challenge of the photographic workshop was on the one hand to create a conceptual approach to manifesting a single visual description capable of describing a motion, and on the other hand to construct the representation of this emotion. Some participants rationalised the mood or impression of an emotion; others worked through spontaneously and intuitively developing a reaction. They considered how they relate to space, ›What meaning can be established or intuited from the space? What values are they confronting or negotiating in their final visual expression?‹ In this way, participating photographers were required to approach their projects as both an act of self expression and an act of producing a set of values concerning human relations and their social and architectonic context, as well as documenting the fabric of social and urban life.«

The photographers involved realised that they were not passive observers, but co-participants in a creative act. They also had to consider questions of how to represent a personal emotion as pure abstraction, and how to extend it into an image of artistic expression. I asked participants to collaborate among themselves by depicting each other's responses, and to collaborate with an audience, in the case of happenings. This demands interaction and provokes an acute awareness (which was sometimes painfully embarrassing or difficult for the participants) of the social nature of public space. By asking the participants to interpret and photograph a personal emotion within a public building as the stage for this subjectification, they were led to question the relationship between personal autonomy, institutional space, and audience.

REFLEXION

»Without introducing the process of a conceptual approach to taking a photograph and therefore producing a sign of the city to the participants, we would end up with a body of work enclosed in the digital system of depicting information and disseminating that information through the system of the web. The key here is the act of photographing rather than the system that exposes the images, all of which works in the service of creating art based not only on communication and instantaneity, but on rigour and substance.«

The participants gained knowledge of the work of contemporary artists and photographers, the dynamics of working in groups and sharing ideas, and ways to photograph the architectonic space of buildings. The group learned how to discuss concepts of identity and how to choose the place within the building in which the photographic session could take place. They became able to negotiate the presence of the public in the building. They learned how to become more autonomous artists, to think for themselves and to confront the issue of working in a public space. One group had to negotiate with the local police about what they were doing and thus realised the complexity of the social rights that exist within the urban setting and how to negotiate them. Psychologically, they were

required to negotiate the subjective messages of government and the social network that brings publics space into being: that they are members of an obedient community, patrolling their own boundaries, aware of authority and of the gaze of other people.

Walking, Talking, Photographing

London Workshop with artist Melissa Bliss

The London Central workshops were organised by FreqOut, an innovative digital arts agency based in Westminster in Central London. Artist Melissa Bliss worked with young people, some of whom were homeless, to take photographs with mobile phones. During the workshops they walked around their local area as a group, telling stories about the area. Here is her report:

BACKGROUND

I am an artist whose work is about people and place, and often about the processes and impacts of urban change. I use different media including photography, video, sound, and live performance. For several years I have worked with young people, often in difficult situations, to use creativity to reach new levels of expression or action. I often use storytelling as a way of reaching into people's experiences. FreqOut puts young people – who may not otherwise get access to digital technologies – together with artists to use emergent technologies to create interesting and innovative projects. They have used wireless technologies, mobile technologies, Bluetooth, GPS tracking, social networking, and CCTV. FreqOut aims to enable young people to be creative, to improve their quality of life, and to break down barriers between communities. It mainly works in Westminster in Central London, an area where extremes of wealth and poverty sit side by side. Westminster is the site of state, church, and royal power in Britain. There is a well-trodden tourist circuit taking in Parliament, Buckingham Palace, Trafalgar Square, the National Gallery, Tate Britain, Leicester Square, and Covent Garden. It is also home to many people; most of whom are working class and live in social housing. There are also a lot of homeless people living on the streets or in temporary hostels – people from London, the rest of Britain, and abroad.

THE WORKSHOP

We invited young people aged fourteen to twenty-five in West-minster to take part in Signs of the City. The older ones were street homeless – living and sleeping on the streets – or living in temporary housing. We met the younger ones through youth clubs. The groups were international – some were from or had parents from Portugal, South Africa, Columbia, Eritrea, Paki-stan, the Caribbean, and Lebanon, as well as Britain – an aver-age London mix. The group had »extreme geographies« – some hardly went out of the area they grew up in while others came from abroad and had travelled great distances. Their perspec-tives are very different to the civil servants, office workers, or tourists in the same streets.

We used mobile phones to take the photographs. I have been using mobile phones with young people for several years – taking photographs, recording sound, shooting and editing films, and sharing work by Bluetooth. I am interested in the differ-ences between photographs taken on mobile phones, on digi-tal cameras, and film cameras – differences in composition, style, technical constraints, and meaning. All the young people I worked with, whatever their age or circumstances, knew how to use mobile phones to take and share photographs and most had their own phones.

We ran five one-day workshops, three at homeless centres and two at youth clubs. Some people came to more than one session. We provided lunch and mobile phones to take photo-graphs. We started by making a communal map of the local area. We laid a big street map on a table and added markers for places that had significance – memories, associations or opinions.

Our main activity was walking – talking – photographing as a group. We went out together and took turns to decide whether we went left, right, or straight ahead. As we walked, we talked about the streets and stories emerged – this was a place where they had come shopping, walked when homeless, argued with their friend. Later we came back to the community centre where we started, ate lunch, and showed everyone's photographs on a slideshow. Then each person selected their best photographs for the Citipix website.

REFLEXION ON PHOTOGRAPHY AND STORIES

The act of walking as a group – when most are used to walking through the streets autonomously – gave a feeling of collective enterprise. We flowed through the streets, talking among our-selves, bringing out different stories, thoughts, and emotions. We went into places that we had not been before – as a way of opening up the city. We took photographs to try to express these thoughts. In the line of Signs of the City, each participant created an avatar with a nickname:

the star 1000 titled his series »the grime behind the glamour in the West End.« He chose to take us down the back streets

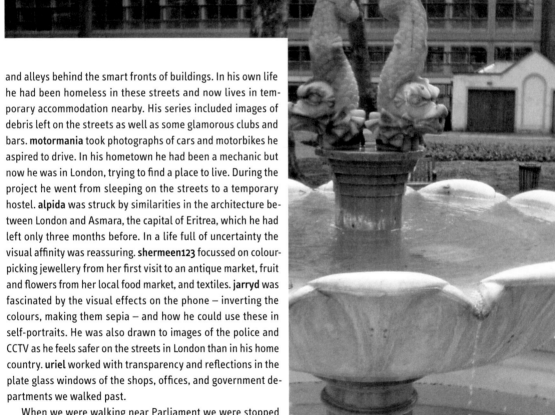

and alleys behind the smart fronts of buildings. In his own life he had been homeless in these streets and now lives in temporary accommodation nearby. His series included images of debris left on the streets as well as some glamorous clubs and bars. **motormania** took photographs of cars and motorbikes he aspired to drive. In his hometown he had been a mechanic but now he was in London, trying to find a place to live. During the project he went from sleeping on the streets to a temporary hostel. **alpida** was struck by similarities in the architecture between London and Asmara, the capital of Eritrea, which he had left only three months before. In a life full of uncertainty the visual affinity was reassuring. **shermeen123** focussed on colour-picking jewellery from her first visit to an antique market, fruit and flowers from her local food market, and textiles. **jarryd** was fascinated by the visual effects on the phone – inverting the colours, making them sepia – and how he could use these in self-portraits. He was also drawn to images of the police and CCTV as he feels safer on the streets in London than in his home country. **uriel** worked with transparency and reflections in the plate glass windows of the shops, offices, and government departments we walked past.

When we were walking near Parliament we were stopped by plain-clothed police. They were nervous about young men taking photographs on their mobile phones in a »security zone.« In case we were terrorists.

London East

Workshop by Douglas Nicolson in conjunction
with SPACE Studios in London

Douglas Nicolson considers himself a community artist. His educational skills combine perfectly in the surroundings of one of London's most contested terrains: Hackney, where city planners dream the Olympic dream. Douglas was able to »highjack« an urban art and education programme for Signs of the City. Here is how he works:

The workshops were held at SPACE studios, a charitable arts organisation in East London, in February 2008. Two workshop programmes took place, each consisting of five sessions. Each session comprised a two-hour slot in the morning or afternoon. The aim was to involve young people aged thirteen to nineteen in a thought-provoking and fun series of mobile, digital media, and photographic activities that mapped Hackney's street life. SPACE gave technical and workshop support with access to a large workshop space, a digital media suite, digital devices such as GPS, a digital media technician, and a volunteer workshop assistant who were both available throughout the project.

Recruitment was handled by SPACE, which approached local community organisations and schools. It was decided to schedule the project to coincide with Hackneys Council's local youth arts week »Discover Young Hackney.« An open call for participants for the project was included in the promotional material advertising DYH.

WORKSHOP

- **Session 1:** Introduction, group forming, discussion.
- **Session 2:** Mapping, finding themes and route, intro to technology, composition / visual skills.
- **Session 3:** Walking route / photo shoot, GPS.
- **Session 4:** Downloading, editing, categorising themes.
- **Session 5:** Uploading, GPS / Googlemap, sharing evaluation

The workshops were open-access so it was not possible to know which and how many participants would attend each session until they arrived. After an introduction to the project to clarify expectations, the group played warm-up games to allow the participants to become comfortable with each other and the working space.

Inviting exploration through doing worked well as the participants started to make mind-maps of their local area from memory. They were encouraged to embellish these maps with events, situations, places, and people that had personal significance for them. Each person then wrote short list poems around their experience of Hackney, examining the five senses.

A large map of the area was then brought forward and parcel labels were distributed so that transfer locations and experiences could be identified through the exercises on one combined map. Discussion around the elements identified brought to light new events and places and these were also added to the large map. Individuals started to identify what they would

like to explore while on their walk of the local area. A consensus as to where in the local area the group should investigate on the photo shoot was reached by designing a journey that passed through the most »tagged« places on the large paper map.

A series of image-based games was introduced next to explore concepts of visual literacy. These included distributing a range of images to small groups and asking them to scale the images from quiet to noisy or sad to happy. This generated some good discussion and the smaller entities shared what they learned with the group as a whole.

A short introduction to composition (rule of thirds, line, light, pattern, colour, etc.) was underlined with visual examples before introducing the cameras and running through the main features that the participants might want to use while out on the shoot. They were then asked to pick a piece of paper »out of the hat« that contained a composition element they had to illustrate with a photograph. The group tried to guess what each other's compositional elements were.

At the next session, everyone walked the route marked on the large paper map together and explored the elements they had identified in their discussions of the short list poems they had created and were of interest to them. The participants were free to explore the space and take any images that they were attracted to, however they were also asked to look for examples of their chosen theme (transport) or object (drain covers). GPS devices were taken on the walk to electronically trace our route.

Back at SPACE studios, the participants downloaded their images onto a workstation and went through a selection process. This involved categorising the images into sub-folders by the subject of the image and selecting examples of the category that they thought worked well. Signs of the City ID cards with the web addresses, usernames, and logons were given to them to try to make it feel as if they were joining something and to help them to remember the details easily.

The selected images were then uploaded onto the Signs of the City website. As the Signs of the City website was still in development at the time and it was not possible to embed GPS data, the GPS data was tagged to the pictures and then exported onto a Google map and displayed on the SPACE website as a companion to the main project.

Reflexion

The images produced were driven by the personal interests of the participants, one person examined drain covers, while another searched for little colourful scraps on the pavement, and another explored the industrial feel of the area by documenting the extractor vents at the back of industrial buildings. Two brothers had an interest in street culture and tried to find and evaluate the best graffiti in the area. It became an investigative, going out to find things; that was their mission, and the things they found were highly individual.

All of the young people were interested in the GPS mapping of their images and engaged in exploring each other's images on the shared map of their local area. As many of the participants chose to document elements that they might not normally take notice of as they move through the city, new perspectives on how their local area can be viewed emerged.

Map of Signs

Workshop with Martin Ruge, Berlin
with KIM Vocational College
(Oberstufenzentrum)

The Berlin-based photographer and graphic designer worked once a week with a group of sixth form students from KIM in Berlin, a secondary school that specialises in communication and media technologies. Martin had already worked on the previous project »Archive of Signs« and other workshops and exhibition projects based on an approach similar to that of the Signs of the City project. Ruge's idea was to create a map of Berlin out of signs, logos, and symbols found in the city. The use of GPS technology added a special attraction to the students of this technical secondary school. At the same time the workshop was designed to be part of a media assistant training scheme, leading to a professional training certificate, thus fitting into the school curriculum.

»I liked working with the young participants and I think that they enjoyed it, too. They were not only interested in looking at my artistic work – I showed them a variety of my photographic works in order to convey my approach – but it was also interesting to them to understand my work as an employee of a photography agency or my personal carrier, which I talked openly about. I think they could relate that to their own potential as their vocational area is close to mine. That helped to generate a trusting atmosphere. I generally tried to convey my approach to work, however the participants had the space and freedom to shape their work individually.« (Martin Ruge in an interview)

WORKSHOP

Equipped with GPS, all of the images that the participants collected were tagged with location coordinates that made up an interactive online map of Berlin. The idea was that the photographers would explore the map, track individual journeys through the city and discover similarities and/or differences between the various districts and neighbourhoods of their city. Within this workshop, the young participants developed a map of Berlin's signs. The workshop explored and documented the sign system of the city using GPS technology and digital cameras. With the help of GPS-loggers, the participants could map the places and sites at which the individual photographs were taken on an online cartography service. The digital photographs were allocated to their places of origination via GPS data in a geo-tagging process and uploaded on to an interactive online map of Berlin. By using this map the city can be read through its signs collected by the workshop participants.

Ruge also used »signs« in a more narrow sense than most of the other artists in the project: »According to my understanding anything can turn into/become a ›sign‹, representing something behind it. In my workshop I limited it to the ›mere sign‹ which is to an extent *dressed* to be a ›sign‹, a label, a pictogram. I like them very much as they often demonstrate quite an aesthetic level; sophisticatedly and radically reduced in terms of line, form, colour, they bring things (meanings/thoughts/messages) to a bare concise point.

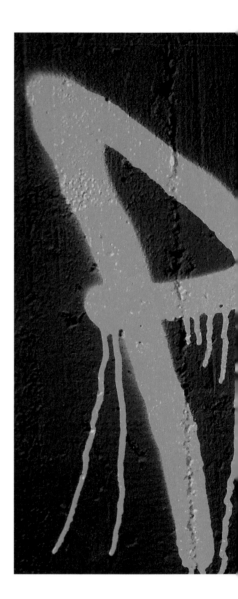

It's astonishing and fascinating that they produce meanings often beyond a particular language/cultural context. It is also sometimes funny and bewildering when you cut the most familiar signs e.g., traffic signs out of their ordinary context, in which they may appear not as ›signs‹ but rather like natural components in a rigid, functional system, you put them into a series or you start playing with them, relating them to other objects.«

Reflexion

According to Alison Rooke, the evaluator of Signs of the City, Ruge's workshop »is an example of how the concepts central to the project, exploring the sign systems of the European city, can be interrogated and worked within a vocational training concept, bringing together artistic practice, technology, and graphic design. Martin's workshop explores the signs system of Berlin as a way of deciphering space and its meaning in an almost archaeological way, by excavating signs, as traces of other times and spheres, removing them from their found context through close-up photography, categorising them via GPS, and examining the sign and its relationship to the place it was found. It is in some ways concerned with creating certain order in the chaos of signs which we are all exposed to as city dwellers.«

Martin Ruge himself was surprised that the participants, to a large extent, followed his working approach to cutting signs off from their contexts and to understanding their figure and composition. However, the participants came up with different results.

»They focussed more on street art, on funny and sometimes absurd messages. I could not have produced this; the photographers used their own fantasy and discovered original signs. I can see my signature (or footprints) in the final output, so certain homogeneity came through but you can see that they have worked on their own.«

After the rules and basic framework had been made clear, the participants increasingly wished to work individually. They were a bit reluctant to work in bigger teams. This could be because of the long way to school for many of the participants and also because of the fact that they were doing their job placements during that period of time. As soon as they discovered that the work could be done individually, at home, on the streets, many of them decided to work on their own.

One technical element became central for their work: the website www.citipix.net. Says Ruge: »It was astonishing how quickly they became acquainted with the server procedures, the uploading. I tried to convey why the server is not just a picture container but supports / requires that you ›frame‹ your photographs, with tagging / wording, that you give personality to your photos, that you enable others to relate to your photos by categorising them, and that you make them trackable with the geo data, etc. I also think that the server represented quite a crucial element of the work – a possible analogue to a concluding exhibition after a work period. The fact that they had to select the best ones out of the many photographs collected, to upload them, tagging / key-wording them, and to show them to the world, was very motivating. They also saw that the website citipix is not an ordinary mass server but a special one, with artistic connotations. It was somehow magnetic, enticing to them. They also worked at home to upload photographs. If their work had no viewer it would not be an ›opus‹; in the best case it would only remain individual fun.«

Freestyle Berlin

Workshop by Britt Hatzius and Stefan Horn
with students from Zukunftsbau, Berlin

U rban dialogues has been working closely with the training and qualification centre Zukunftsbau since September 2006. Based on the educational concept that underlies Signs of the City, Zukunftsbau conducted four projects, each with fifteen unemployed young people between the ages of seventeen and twenty-five. The projects were realised under a German training scheme for the unemployed, in which the participants received financial compensation (in this case EUR 200 per month) in addition to their unemployment benefit if they engaged in specific training schemes or short-term job opportunities that might make their return to the labour market more likely (*Arbeitsgelegenheiten mit Mehraufwandsentschädigung*, MAE). Within the framework of the Signs of the City project, and under this German scheme, the media Lab at Zukunftsbau ran a course on photography and digital media skills in cooperation with two Berlin job centres (Friedrichshain-Kreuzberg and Pankow). Participants were given the opportunity to attend occupational training sessions and thus attain a vocational qualification in these subjects over a period of nine to twelve months. Artistic work is supported by the European Social Fund (ESF) through the »New Jobs and Education Programme.«

WORKSHOP

The courses, with fifteen participants each, were based on three main elements. The participants were given professional guidance in writing and developing job applications and targeting adequate professional career options, and were offered professional work experience for up to three months, according to their occupational preferences. They performed community work in a freely chosen field, thus attaining concrete insight into the potentials and realities of the working environment.

Based on the core concept of Signs of the City, the third element was creative work with professional artists on urban photography. The course not only sought to teach participants hands-on technical and artistic skills, but also to help them to acquire new visual competence and heighten their awareness of the urban environment.

This third element was further subdivided into three main areas of activity: The course sought to transmit basic skills related to digital photography and the post-production of digital images using common graphic design software.

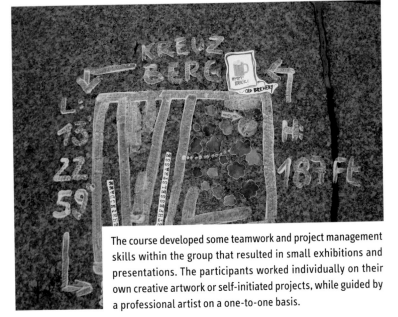

The course developed some teamwork and project management skills within the group that resulted in small exhibitions and presentations. The participants worked individually on their own creative artwork or self-initiated projects, while guided by a professional artist on a one-to-one basis.

REFLEXION

Compared with international standards, these programmes may seem to be paradise for unemployed young people. In everyday reality, however, they are often more about a dogged struggle with the participants. Many of the participating young people suffer from the effects of a now outdated school system; they lack social competences and find it difficult to stick to a regular schedule of attendance and an everyday routine. They usually think of themselves as having lost out in a system that constantly circles around them – a system of state institutions, employment agencies, and professional facilitators, which seems in their view to obstruct their personal development. Consequently, the turnover of the participants over the course of one year was relatively high. Needless to say, this also raised problems for the facilitators in charge of curricular planning and delivery.

These recurring difficulties notwithstanding, the courses left a measurable and lasting impact on many participants.

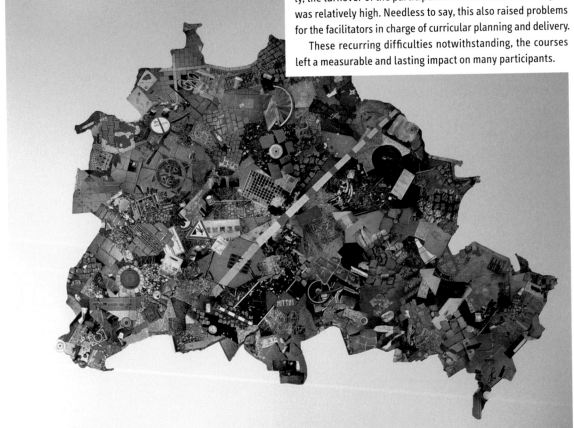

»For me a lot has changed in my perception of the city. The aesthetics of tristesse has become very personal to me. I am an urban child. These things are very close to me. I like Berlin a lot because it builds on two systems; one against the other. It has its own dynamic in contrast to Hamburg for example which is a master plan. Berlin is a monster; it cannot be tamed.«

Some young people came to the project with the objective of kick-starting a creative professional career. They encountered a safe haven, in which they could prepare for the qualifying exams of design academies or photography schools.

»My attitude changed. I could expose myself to things, look at new things, what attracts me, what not. At the beginning it was clear: timeframe 9.30–15.30. I adapted to it. Then it became less set, I adapted myself to that, too. Now I'm open, I don't mind what I do (in the future), It was good to have done that. The project meant more to me personally than my student time. I found the people here more interesting than the students at the university. If you think of the unemployed they are usually the losers, but that was not the case here. People here have potential, self initiative, they are agile people. I like to work with them, not with students.«

Other participants found the methodological constellation of creative education, concrete project development, and individual guidance useful for gaining access to other professional careers. In any case they all made significant progress in terms of their personal development, as they became aware of their own ideas and skills and learned to reflect on them.

»The positive to me was that I could make photography not only documentation, but expression of myself.« The long duration of the project certainly allowed the facilitators to coach each participant individually. As a result, many of the end results could become complex and multifaceted pieces of work that were developed and guided over a period of several months.

The Young People and their Place in the City – Point of View and History

An overview of the local project in Sofia
by Velislava Donkina, Milkana Lazarova, Ivan Kiruanov and Andrei Rashev,
Atelier for Free Associations

At the very beginning, when we started to gather a group for the first workshop, we thought a lot about what would be important for the young people aged between fifteen and twenty-six, who might be interested in taking part in this project. We had an idea of creating a free space focussing on personality, personal histories of life – not in its biographical or chronological sense, but rather on how we see ourselves, what we think about who we actually are and where we are situated within the recent events of our lives. Topics such as the relationship between the young person and the city, symbols and spaces of the megapolis and how we react to them, personal desire, the personal search for sense were of great importance to us. We wanted to be different to similar projects in Bulgaria, which seemed to be doing too much acting, and not enough listening and asking as to where exactly the real and deep meaning of such work can be found.

THE WORKSHOP

With that in mind, we left the opportunity of taking part in the workshop open. That meant that we distributed information about the project around Sofia and we made it possible for anyone who was interested to make a phone call and arrange a personal appointment at a time, which would be convenient for him/her.

We introduced ourselves to each other at these meetings, which were individual, and explained who we were and what this project was about; who was involved and who was organising it. We encouraged the young people to tell us about their interests and wishes, about their expectations and about how they saw the opportunity to join the workshops as places for debate and exchange of thoughts and ideas.

These meetings were led by the psychologist who works in the workshop and sometimes by the local manager of the project for Sofia. The artists also became involved by moderating

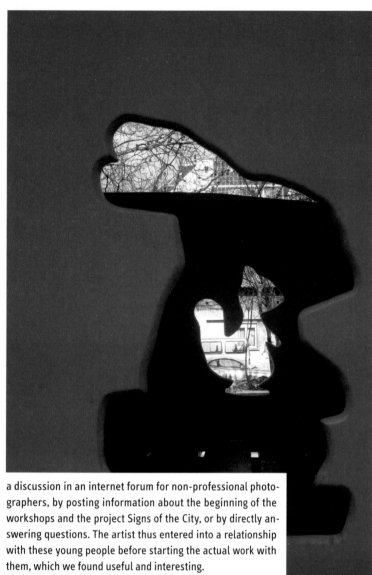

a discussion in an internet forum for non-professional photographers, by posting information about the beginning of the workshops and the project Signs of the City, or by directly answering questions. The artist thus entered into a relationship with these young people before starting the actual work with them, which we found useful and interesting.

At the same time everyone came with their own desires and personal questions. For one participant this meant looking for sense in a picture that is technically of a very high standard, seeking pleasure in doing something. For someone else, a girl with a boyfriend who enjoyed taking pictures and wanted to become a famous photographer, this workshop was a way of doing something for her relationship, of being able to spend more time with her partner by supporting him in something that he liked and of becoming more interesting and important to him. They operated their relationship within the working space; they arrived together and had quarrels there, she left and then came back again. In the end the artist leading the project discovered that she actually took much better pictures than he did, perhaps because of the pleasure that she found in doing that.

Our workshop structure was four working groups during the period of the project with five to ten people in each group. They met twice a week for two hours over a two-month period.

Two artists led the groups and three psychologists held the individual meetings, group discussions, and closing sessions. That meant that we had one artist and one psychologist as a facilitator for each group, providing supervision of the process by a therapist with experience of working with teenagers.

We also had the opportunity to invite special guests; experts, who work on the topic »city« participated in the workshop and also initiated debates.

The types of groups and the ways in which they came together were very interesting. The first were young people who were interested in professional photography. We later discovered that the young people, who had already met anonymously on the internet forum using nicknames and spent the first workshop meetings arguing and continuing disputes that began in the internet, had begun to use the workshop as a special area. Such areas are termed »transitional spaces« by the British psychoanalyst Donald Winnicotte; safe and steady space, where one could come regularly or sporadically for no apparent reason, to chat, to leave something such as ideas and thoughts, to take something left by another, to accept or to work out certain issues, and then to leave. The second group comprised young painters.

The group for the third atelier in Sofia was made up of participants who had wanted to join the project a long time ago, but for various reasons hadn't managed to do so. They were joined by others who had been told of the workshops by friends who had taken part in the first two workshops. Most of them were still at school and had no previous experience of photography. The members of the fourth group were young participants with individual projects. This was a very interesting group. As there were so few volunteers, we decided to make it a lab for individual projects.

REFLEXION

The difficult period of puberty features specific psychological states of being that lead young people to want to be heard, yet at the same time to not want it. For that reason personal histories – in pictures, ideas, words, comings and goings from the workshop – were of great importance to us. We tried to be there to listen to the young men and women while they searched for themselves in their city and asked such questions as, »Why is the face of the city that way? Do we make symbols in our lives or do we just receive them from someone else? Do we have the opportunity or responsibility to create?«

It is always important to have a specific framework when working with groups. Without it the work is impossible, however when teenagers are involved it must be soft and flexible. We tried to put the frames of work into the material – the pictures, the words, into finding the pleasure of making art, into doing something, into finding things out, into sharing with others, into trying to understand what you see, into communicating through pictures, into being inspired, into making your own exhibition, as the participants did a few days ago; to be the author of your own ideas of life and the city you live in no matter where on earth that is.

LAB 2 – Barcelona

chapter two

Exchange Programme LAB2

6–10 October 2008 in Barcelona

A travelogue compiled by Stefan Horn,
Artistic Director, urban dialogues, Berlin

THE AIM

The aim of the Barcelona LAB2 encounter was to gather photographers and artists to explore city life and advance their photographic skills. It focused on a multilevel dialogue about differences and commonalities in the participating cities. It was based on a common interest and passion to share cross-city and cross-country experiences and perspectives. The images produced during the gathering in Barcelona were an occasion for deeper reflection and discussion about city life, from the participants point of view.

How do I see the previously unknown city of Barcelona? What suits my expectations and what surprises me? What are the differences to my own city? How can I communicate these differences? Are there commonalities too? Would I like to live in one of the other cities?

PARTICIPANTS

A group of fifteen young photographers from London, Berlin and Sofia took part in this exchange program. They met different school classes and a group of young immigrants in Barcelona to share ideas, knowledge, and skills around photographic research in urban space. All of them had already attended a previous workshop before they set off for Barcelona. These young urban photographers were guided by nine artists altogether, from the different cities, to carry out different exploratory workshops. The evaluation team from the Centre for Urban and Community Research, Goldsmiths College, University of London and the coordinator of the leading organisation urban dialogues also attended the five-day gathering. Beside the workshop sessions there was plenty of time to enjoy the city of Barcelona and do things on their own. All participants had the chance to explore the city, individually and in teams, upload their photographic findings online (research sessions), meet each other, and connect and share experience (round tables). At the beginning, participants were divided into four workshop groups, guided by supporting artists, engaging in different activities. In the end, a closing session provided the oppurtunity to have a look back on the outcomes and process of this encounter.

Check-In

SATURDAY 4 OCT
Sofia Group
16.40 Departure from Sofia
18.50 Arrival in Barcelona
Bulgaria Air Nr. 477
Accomodation Sofia Group
Hostal Fernando
Carrer de Ferran 31
www.hfernando.com
Barri Gòtic

SUNDAY 5 OCT
Berlin Group
08.25 Departure from Berlin Schönefeld
11.00 Arrival in Barcelona Easyjet and
14.00 Departure from Berlin Tegel
16.30 Arrival in Barcelona Click Air
Accomodation Berlin Group
Hostal Levante
Baixada de Sant Miquel 2
www.hostallevante.com
Barri Gòtic

SUNDAY 5 OCT
London Group
10.55 Departure from London Gatwick
14.00 Arrival in Barcelona
Accomodation London Group
Apartment Address: Ginebra, 28
http://www.gobcn.com/BARCELONA_PLAYA/Barcelona_playa.htm
Barceloneta

The Core of LAB2 in Barcelona

1_Exploring the unknown city of Barcelona

2_Producing and sharing photographic work on the spot

3_Deepening the workshop experiences so far

4_Discussing experiences of city life

5_Sharing ideas about creative ways to capture the city

6_Discussing differences and commonalities between the four cities

Copy Me – LAB 2, October 2008

INTRO

The game Copy Me has been conceived for Signs of the City. The aim is to play a performative game, using purely visual exchange to compare the four cities participating in Signs of the City.

TODAY

Today we want to make a new version, to »copy«, one single image of Berlin. Is it possible to copy a photograph? Is it possible to re-create a photograph from another city, here in Barcelona? We don't want to just take a photograph of the same item thats in the photograph. E.g., if there's a coffee cup, don't necessarily photograph a coffee cup.

The first exercise is describing a photo using the following categories:

- **Formal.** Proportion, structure, shapes etc.
- **Colour and Light.** Daylight or electric? Dark or bright? What colours?
- **Content/Subject.** What is »in« the photograph? Which objects? What is happening?
- **Message/Statement.** What does the photographer want to say? What is the photo saying? Positive or negative?

After this, we can use one of these categories to try and »copy« the photo today.

Obviously the categories can be blurred, but to seperate these out is an attempt to try different ways to make a new version of a photograph. Otherwise there is an understandable tendency to look for visual patterns, such as circles or blocks of colour. This is interesting, but a more complex visual comparison could be acheived. Thats the aim at least!

THIS WEEK

Participants from all four cities involved in Signs of the City will copy this photograph.

AFTER THIS WEEK

We will try to find a day when participants from all four cities can copy a photograph simultaneously. The team that makes the »best« copy will choose the next photograph to be copied by all the other cities.

Oliver

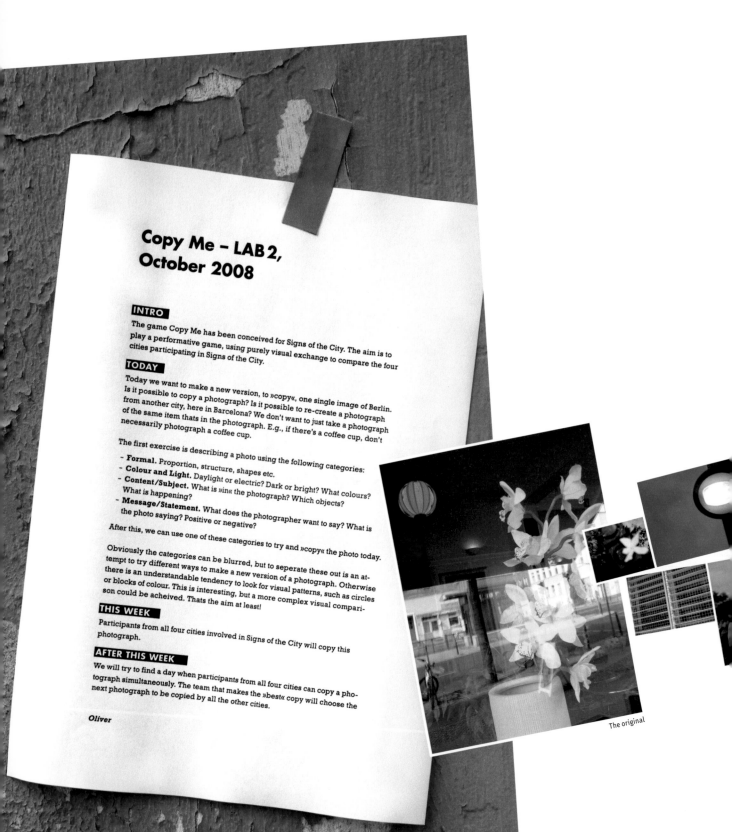

The original

OLIVER WALKER

(talking about the group of young participants from London)
»Maybe they have never been to Liverpool and if they did go to Liverpool, they would be like 'ah this is a corner of the UK I have never seen before, but it is still my country. The question is whether, when they come to Barcelona, they somehow feel connected? Maybe the best way to make them feel European would be to send them to Texas!«

Workshop by Oliver Walker, Berlin-based Artist

The copies

Acting Together

WORKSHOP IDEA FROM PAULA KLEIMAN,
BARCELONA-BASED ARTIST:

Mapa personal de Trinitat Vella *Personal map*
1_Mi sitio favorito para quedar con amigos
My favorite place to stay with friends
2_Para una cita romantica *For a date*
3_Un lugar donde haya pasado algo importante en mi vida
A place that is important in my life's history
4_Cosas que me llaman la atención en el camino de casa al cole
Things I used to see on my way from home to school
5_Un sitio que del que tengas un mal recuerdo
A place that evokes a bad memory
6_Un sitio donde puedas ir a desconectar
A place where you might go to disconnect
7_Una buena vista de la ciudad *A nice view of the city*

WORKSHOP IDEA FROM TEREZ OSZTAFI,
LONDON-BASED ARTIST:

Young people from Barcelona show young people from London special places, locations that have a special meaning to them. Maybe something specific happened in that spot, i.e., first kiss, a minor accident, grandma's house, cat was run over, positive or negative experience, something significant to them personally. Paula could give the Barcelona children a mini-questionnaire and a map where they could mark this place in their local area and take the Londoners there. This tour would be recorded photographically.

What's Europe?

Paula Kleiman:
»Today Sara from Trinidat Vella asked Nuria, ›What's Europe?‹ she has lived here all her life, it is an indication that something has happened.«

Nuria Calafell:
»And she doesn't know if England is European or part of the United States.«

Erica Scourti:
»This is a very good question though; because England isn't really Europe, is it? Mentally I don't think it is.«

Terez Osztafi:
»You say I am going to Europe on holiday.«

Erica Scourti:
»So you say, but you are in Europe, yeah but you know what I mean. There is Europe and there is England.«

Statement

by Andrei Rashev, Sofia-based Photographer

LAB2 in Barcelona was a very interesting exchange program, and we are very happy to have been able to take part in this additional workshop. The idea of mixing different cultural types, from four different cities was amazing.

For our group, Barcelona was a totally unknown city. None of us had ever been to Spain before. Our main idea was to explore the city, to find these different types of culture. Searching for unique signs, signs that are typical only to this city. Barcelona is a very old city and has very interesting old parts and quarters. It is difficult to discover the entire city in only five workdays, so we had a tight schedule: looking at the old part of Barcelona, exploring the new parts of the city, trying to find the real life in the city, talking to people, and running away from tourist zones. Of course visiting landmarks of the city is necessary from a cultural point of view – for example, the architecture of Gaudi houses is unique. But we also had the opportunity to compare two very typical and very different quarters – La Barceloneta and La Gracia. The real life in those two areas was very impressive. You could see both very poor and very rich people, the kids playing in the streets and gardens, old people sitting on benches discussing different aspects of life, and having long conversations in the cafes. At one point or other, each one of us would say – »wow! time here seems as if it stops« and this is the true somehow.

The second element of our work was to create a stripe of photographs. I think this was an interesting part of exploring the city, because you can start working on a theme. And you can search for signs in different parts of the city, and combine them into a series to create your own interpretations of those signs.

The third element was the most experimental part of our work. GPS technology was new for us. In the near future though, they will be playing large roles in our lives. You can tag every place. We are only at the beginning of the Google Earth era, which will surely be deeply integrated in our lives in the next ten years.

To conclude, I can say that LAB2 really was an incredibly impressive project for everybody from Sofia. Everyone in the group was able to express different points of view through discovering the signs of Barcelona.

MARTA FROM SOFIA:

»Funny things that happened: We were walking with a friend, and while taking photos we saw a sign with a sleeping man with ›z-z-z-z-z‹ written on it. We asked a Spanish woman what the sign meant. She thought we didn't have a place to sleep and told us about the nearest hotel. She was very kind. After that, we understood that the sign meant: ›be quiet, there are sleeping men around!‹ It was very funny.«

Check-Out

SATURDAY 11 OCT

Berlin Group
Departure 10.40 Barcelona
Arrival 13.20 Berlin

Sofia Group
Departure 19.10 Barcelona
Arrival 22.55 in Sofia

London Group
Departure 14.30 Barcelona
Arrival London Gatwick 15.50

CHIRAG FROM LONDON:

»Coming from West London and seeing all the graffiti down there is totally different. You don't see different kinds of art as you do here. Seeing real big pieces of art stuck somewhere on the wall makes the place look better in a way. In West London you mainly get tagging or smiley faces, down here you get pictures of birds or people's faces, like in the graffiti artistic way, I'd say the graffiti down here is better than the graffiti we have where we live.«

DOMINIK FROM BERLIN:

»My first impression of Barcelona was – Wow ... a lot of bicycles here. Tourists are everywhere; I don't know who is a real Spanish person and who's the tourist? I like the city. All those old buildings looking so beautiful, I like that. What can I write about the people who live there? A little bit strange, you can see drugs and alcohol everywhere in the small streets. The weather is fantastic. One point I should make is that Barcelona is a little bit expensive, but who cares about that? I'm a photography tourist, that's all.«

Exhibitions

BARCELONA
Can Basté
9 October – 8 November 2008

BERLIN
House of World Cultures
26 September – 2 November 2008

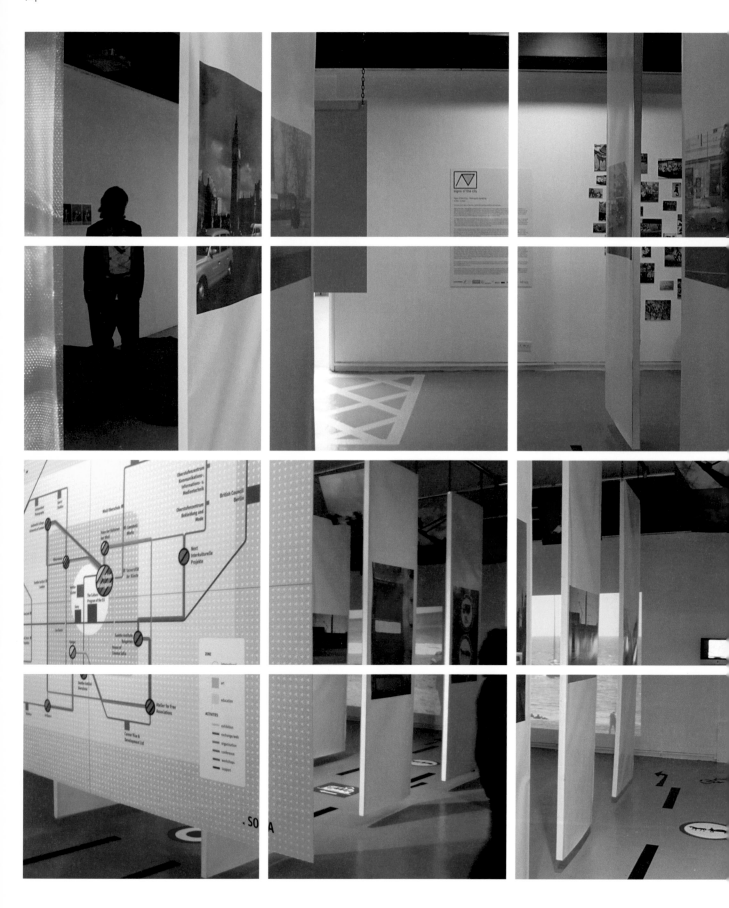

LONDON
Watermans Gallery
4 October – 2 November 2008

SOFIA
Cinema House
15 October –15 November 2008

Pictures

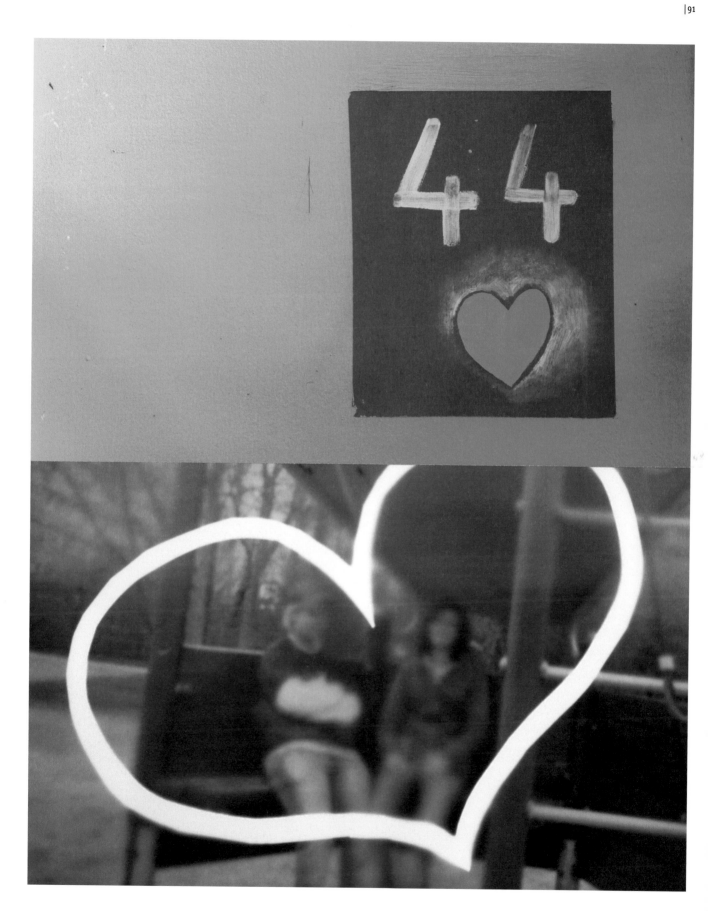

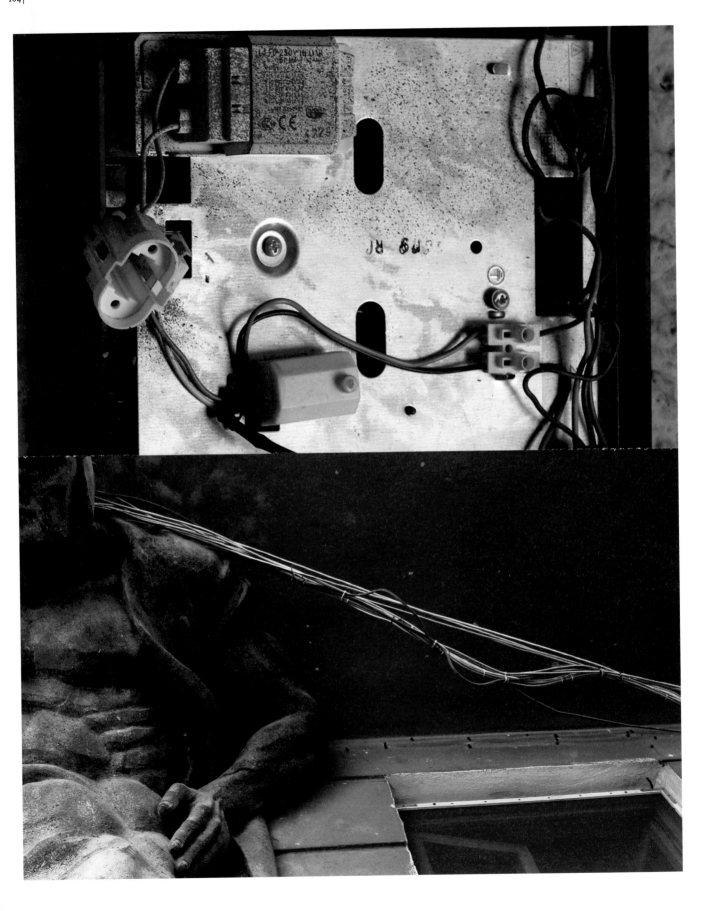

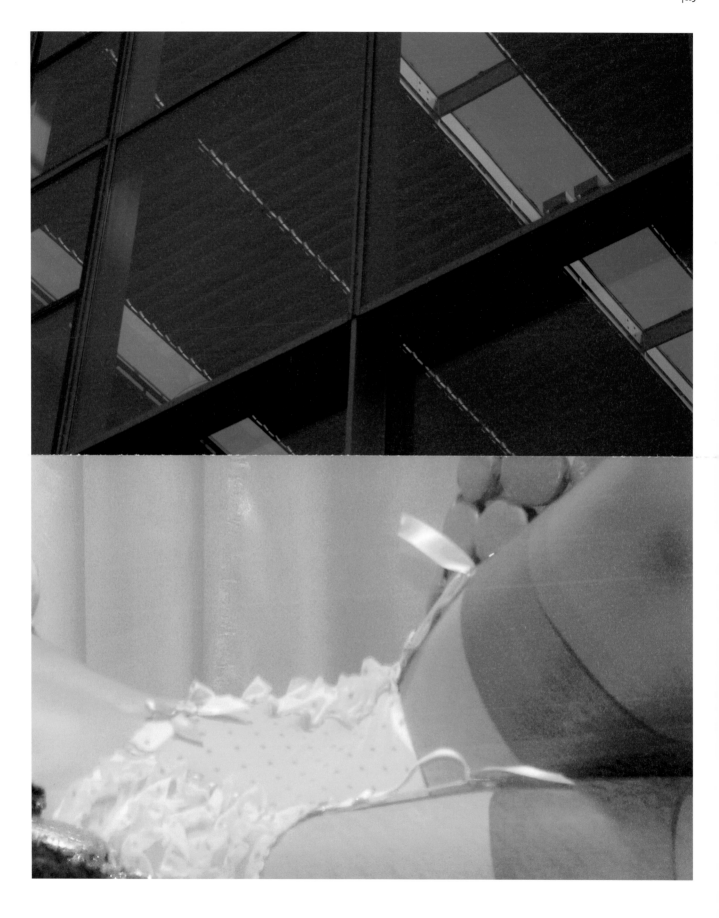

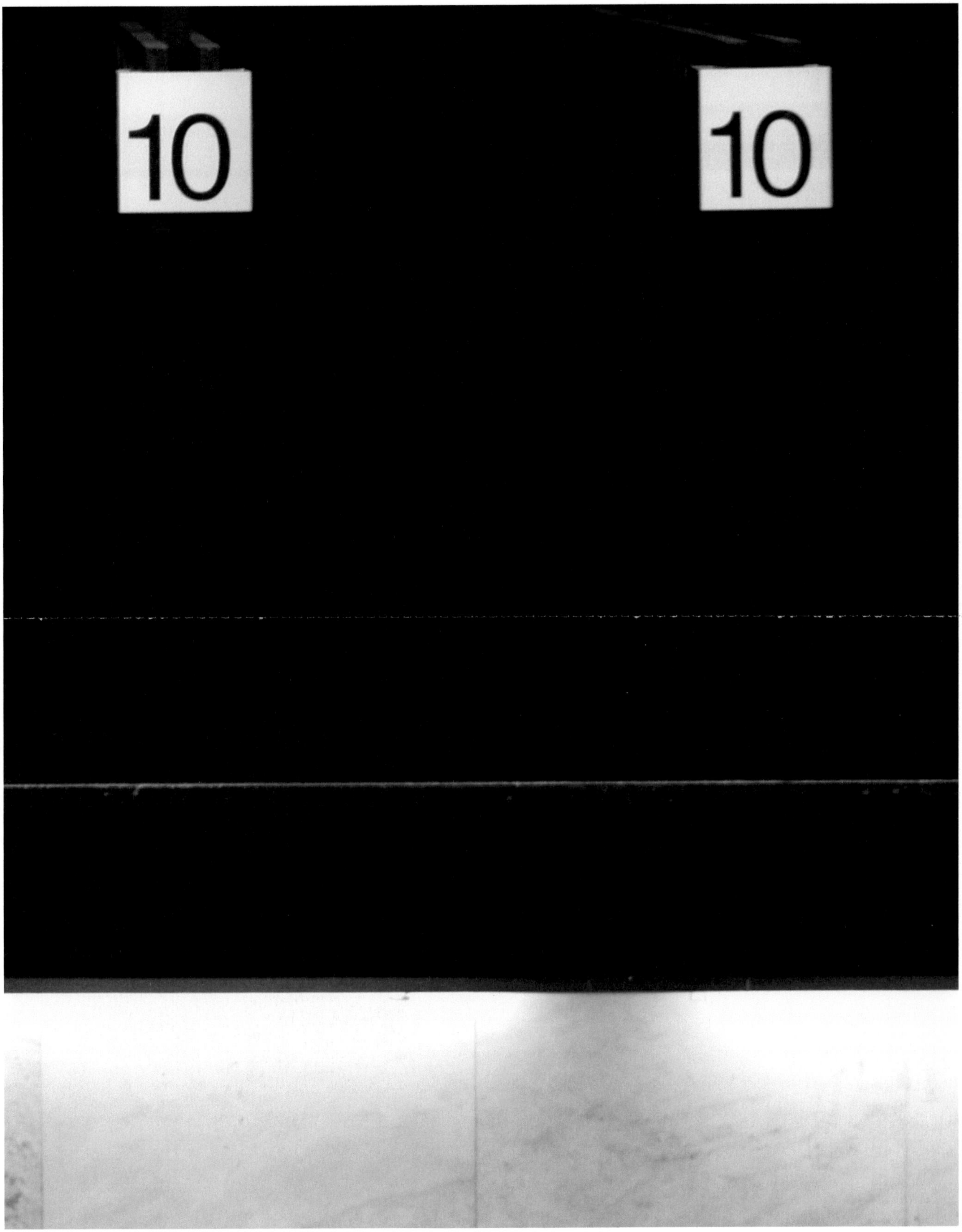
10
10

Conference

chapter five

Signs, my City, Dialogues

Twenty-first Century Urbanism from the Rational to the Relational

by Prof. Michael Keith, Head of the Centre for Urban and Community Research, Goldsmiths College, University of London

METROPOLIS SPEAKING TO THE STRANGELY FAMILIAR CITY

The arrival of modernity and the advent of the modern city closely overlapped each other in the European west. Because many of the modernist arts movements, much of what we understand today as mass culture and the struggles of mode politics were all closely associated with the major economic and social transformations to the way we lived, which resulted from industrialisation and the development of new forms of urban life. For the sociologist Georg Simmel, the modern city was differentiated from its predecessor principally by its sensory overload of noises, sights, smells, crowds, and sensations. The sensorium of the city overwhelmed the person that arrived for the first time in the metropolis. Just as the eye transforms visual sensory data into comprehensible form, to make sense of the excess of information, the urban novice had to rationalise its content, simplify its complexity, and find a way to make the signs of the city legible. Consequently, for Simmel the »rational« was closely related to this editing process; the metropolis characterised by new ways of being, thinking, and doing that could be traced back to this process.

And if the industrial cities of the nineteenth century overwhelmed the spectator, what would Simmel say about the extraordinary megacites of the twenty-first, characterised by time space compression, vast populations, uncertain boundaries, virtual realities, incommensurable worlds of global diasporas and entrenched territorialisation. If the city of the twentieth century attempted to know itself, to rationalise its streets and to plan its future, then perhaps the metropolis of the twenty-first is both more immense and more modest. Creative destruction and socialist reconstruction marked the metropolitan hubris of west and east alike in the recent past, but the utopian transformations of the last century have been significantly discredited.

Today, cultures simultaneously knit a global network, and construct a neighbourhood sensibility; the flows of capital and labour coalesce momentarily in urban form but link nationally and transnationally. Technology transforms humanity and the habitus of the city; mobile phones, the internet, CCTV cameras, the televisual, screens trackers, and GPS systems—all make their users part human, part object—mundanely metropolitan cyborgs. In this world, the link between objects and humans, materialities and subjectivities foregrounds the city's pluralisation. In part this is *the networked city* but a vocabulary of networks does not quite capture the folds, movements, mutability, and reconfigurations of people and infrastructure, or in Maliq Simone's evocative description of the African city of »people as infrastructure«. The whole city becomes more a political imaginary than a socioeconomic form; a horizon of possibility that may structure the actions of social movements and political institutions alike, but cannot be reconciled with the pace of change of an object on the ground that is forever in flux. In this sense »the rational city« of classic modernity is displaced by something more partial, »the relational city« city of today's modernity. In this metropolis, the attempt to dwell or to make a home is always about something slightly precarious, invoking the past, imagining the future, but always recognising that the control of history and geography comes most easily to the powerful, the affluent, and those whose life path is most secure.

The Signs of the City project spoke to this contemporary metropolis in language mediated by the visual practises and performances of the photographic. It also listened, watched, heard and thought about how young people in today's Europe make a space for themselves in the city, try to excavate from the turbulence of the credit crunch, and the burden of socialisation, the banal authoritarianism of racism, and the general invocation to conform a relationship between place, space, and identity that was recognisably their own.

In contrast, the fragments of the conventional city stand metaphorically for a set of narratives that represent the suspect stories of contemporary urbanism. The iconographies of Gaudi's cathedral, Trafalgar Square, Sofia's civic monuments, or Berlin's Alexanderplatz speak to the received wisdoms of the city. In the *Bildungsroman* all these iconographies trace and space; the novice arrives in the metropolis, narrating themselves through exploring the city. In the classic Victorian novel, a movement through the city reflects the moral geography of the urban and its protagonists. Oscar Wilde's Dorian Gray debauches in the east end of the city while the rational, organised, civilised spaces of the west end describe his surface appearance. Linking different worlds through exploring urban form became the architecture of the fictional works of Dickens and Hugo as much as the sociological logics of Engels or DuBois. But these stories quickly become tired, received wisdom becomes caricature or develops an orientalised cartography that makes the city comprehensible only by abusing its complexities and contradictions.

The signs of the street are more complex than these geographical tropes and the reassuring narratives they promote. In a street in Barcelona in 2008, the sign *No Pakis – No Party* appears to evidence everyday racism until you speak to people locally and the intertextual reference to the Martini advertisement campaign (*No Martini – No Party*) is fused with the transgression of the city's regulation of presence in the public sphere. Local government tried to clamp down on open street parties, serviced by migrant Pakistani communities selling liquor. The racist sign in reality is more ambivalent, uncovering a new mythology and a contemporary politics that mediate local cultures and urban politics, drawing on meanings that are globally broadcast and linguistically specific to particular parts of the transgressive city.

MY CITY

»The trope of the palimpsest is inherently literary and tied to writing, but it can also be fruitfully used to discuss configurations of urban spaces and their unfolding in time without making architecture and the city simply into text.« Andreas Huyssen, 2003

The project was developed in four very different cities. Obviously the economic, social, and political trajectories of Barcelona, Berlin, London, and Sofia differ enormously. Likewise, so do the demographics of inclusion and exclusion, migration and settlement.

But in each city, the sense in which artists worked with young people through the medium of the photograph curated both the neighbourhood and representations of the city at large. It provided a powerful axis through which the research project intervened in urban form, identity, and space mediated by very different experiments in photographic practice. Conventional tropes of the four cities were reconfigured by these alternative curations, the hidden disclosed, the visible reconfigured.

There is a way in which the project draws on a sense of the spatial sublime. Where Burke highlighted how a quick transition from darkness to light, »produces an effect on the mind that is even more powerful«, Lyotard famously transformed the sublime into an »event,« with spatial configurations that draw on an urban sensibility: »(...) a movement out of the notional ›we‹ that governs most things in social life and establishes ›the event‹ as outside any formulation of the normal.« In this sense »normal« implies a real perspective, a real place, and a real history. The forgetfulness required by the event, on the other hand, for good or ill, must sublate all three.

The manner in which the photography of young people told the stories of the city differently, the artist's practices reconfigured both representational conventions and the presence of the photographer, draws on and works with the city's own power to confound expectations through an ability to shock, to provoke and to link spaces and create new geometries of the urban, reconstitute new metropolitan imaginaries. This in turn speaks to an urbanism of *the relational aesthetic* in the spirit of a twenty-first century Simmel, a notion that we might borrow from Bourriaud's description of artwork as social interstice:

»The possibility of a relational art, points to a radical upheaval of the aesthetic, cultural and political goals introduced by modern art. To sketch a sociology of this, this evolution stems essentially from the birth of a worldwide urban culture, and from the extension of this city model to more or less all cultural phenomena.«
Relational Aesthetics, Nicolas Bourriaud, 1998

DIALOGUES: SPEAKING EUROPEAN

The work of Signs of the City was ambitious and it was frequently the case that the process of engagement was, if anything, more important. It drew on very different ethical and political traditions of participatory in arts. Between autonomists, *arte povera*, conventions of psychotherapy, and rhetorics of empowerment diffuse practices and traditions characterised each of the four cities involved in the project. The links with training and employment (particularly in Germany) or with civic association and political movement (particularly in Spain) varied similarly. Most significantly, the practices of individual artists shaped the dialogues that were prompted by the project in each of the neighbourhoods where work took place.

At times the photograph in this context might be less a representation than *an interruption* in the visual repertoires of the city. Artists and students described how in Barcelona they might place a picture frame in well-known parts of the city where they would rarely venture, photographing the frame as device (*dispositif*) and a metaphor. The very act of framing the strangely familiar parts of the city opens up a different sort of dialogue. A flamenco guitar in an image asserts the centrality of a Roma presence that is normally marginal to the city. *(pic. 1)*

A presence inside the frame of a self-portrait that takes its content from an ecological sensibility and a fashion cliché can produce an image of dubious aesthetic value and significant social content. *(pic. 2)*

But equally there are moments of beauty in these images that capture a sense of the aesthetics of a relational urbanism. For Kant the horror of the sublime was linked to »an oscillation between fragmentary detail and a notional totality« and the spatial sublime of these images both decodes the signs of the city and opens an imaginary alternative metropolis. In London homeless people pointed the camera back at those who monitor their activity, returning the gaze of surveillance. A self-indulgent client at a beautician is shocked by the cheek of it. The statues of the great and the good look differs from the angle of the streets on which you sleep. Vertiginous buildings query the city horizon. *(pic. 3)*

The presence of two spectral shadows in a space that was normally thought of as too dangerous to enter, play with the binaries of the visible and the invisible city. *(pic. 4)*

Simultaneously they speak to a hope of something different, an alternative urbanism that is always about other times and other places. Significantly, whilst differences in arts practise, participants' work, and the quality of both varied greatly it is nevertheless possible to identify through the formal evaluation of the project and the curated exhibitions that a strong sense of neighbourhood and transnationalism was not always matched by strong identities at the level of the national or the European.

The temporal dimensions of these patterns of glocalisation were also commonly present, most clearly evinced in asset of images that focused on an internet telephone service, linking Barcelona to the diasporic geographies of the city. The temporality of the »elsewhere of place« again triggers a contemporary cartography and a relational temporality.

Conclusion : The Dynamics of Contemporary Urbanism, the Pragmatics of Participatory Arts

Clearly, not all aspects of the Signs of the City project worked, nor was all the photography of a particularly high quality if measured by aesthetic qualities alone. But the work was funded as part of a European initiative that challenged the relationship between arts practice, European identity, and the social configurations of contemporary urbanism.

At its best, it displayed the sort of relational aesthetics identified with Bourriaud, a theorist who in foregrounding the interplay of urbanism, curation, and aesthetics has opened up arts practice in the last decade through articulating a more modest ambition for the artist. He has championed *»the historical chance whereby most of the art worlds known to us managed to spread their wings. ... This chance can be summed up in just a few words: learning to inhabit the world in a better way, instead of trying to construct it based on a preconceived idea of historical evolution.«*

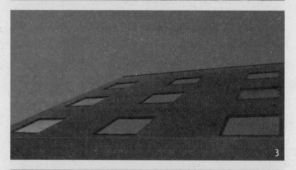

For Bourriaud the relational aesthetic is premised on the sense in which the world on the move echoes de Certeau's notion that we might recognise ourselves as tenants of culture. At its best, the interruptions in the signs of the metropolis provoked by young people on the Signs of the City linked this sense of the relational aesthetic to a relational urbanism. The mirage of the whole city and the refiguration of the subcultural metropolitan fragment are simultaneously realised, even as time past and time present points to one end; which is always present.

Attention!

Signs of the City between Automaticity and Conscious

by Dr. Kristin Veel, Department of Arts and Cultural Studies,
University of Copenhagen

In the twentieth century, Walter Benjamin famously characterised the experience of the modern metropolis as an experience of shock. He also characterised the cinema as embodying these shock effects by presenting subsequent rows of images without giving the viewer time to »contemplate« the individual image. In a similar manner it can be argued that the database documenting the project Signs of the City exposes and problematises the current conditions of information processing and the affinity with the contemporary digitally wired cyber city. This article aims to explore Signs of the City in the light of questions of information processing and attention. How can space for conscious focussed attention and contemplation arise – in the city and in a digital environment? Signs of the City articulates an intriguing discussion of these questions.

The concept of attention belongs in an extensive field of research, which is today highly dominated by neuroscientific research. The brain is regarded by many neuroscientists as a self-organising autopoietic machinery, in which the inner structure of the receiver processes incoming stimuli, whereas there are different opinions on the degree to which neural networks are determined by use and learning. Approximately 90% of our consciousness is currently regarded as functioning through more or less automated processes, while only 10% can be described as conscious focussed attention. Interestingly, new media are often designed to converge with our automatic machinery. The interfaces of mobile phones, PDAs, and mp3 players are not directed towards our conscious attentiveness, but are designed to enter into dialogue with our consciousness' ability to automatically understand and react quickly on signals.

It is simply not desirable if these technologies require serious contemplation in order to be functional. In her recent book, *Echo Objects*, art historian Barbara Maria Stafford raises concerns about this convergence between technology and our automatic machinery. She opposes the tendency to regard visual perception as an automatic response to stimuli and will as an illusion, and opens the possibility of finding creativity in the ability to escape rather than give in to our automatic machinery. In particular, if she calls for a focus on »the remaining nonautopoietic 10 % of the self actively fashioned by, and open to, sensory input coming from the environment.«

Signs of the City situates itself in the very centre of this oscillation between attention and automaticity. As we shall see, on the one hand it carves out a position between using digital technology, which is designed to be easily understandable and help us make sense of the environment (be it the city or the digital database), and on the other hand the project also displays a clear intention to create space for personal engagement with the environment in a way that requires conscious focussed attention. Let us look in more detail at how this ne-gotiation is played out in the project: A key entrance point for someone wanting to access the project Signs of the City is the website www.citipix.net, which features a database and an on-line photo community.

Although the initial experience of the database might be slightly overwhelming due to the amount of images, this data-base is designed in a way, that allows us to navigate the imag-es and acquire access to the information linked to each image without great effort.

The experience is, however, further complicated if we fol-low the interface's invitation to select five images and save them in an individual stripe, which can be given a title. The in-terface offers several options to narrow the selection, and a stripe may well be put together without much effort if we let ourselves be guided by the parameters that the interface gives us. The search parameters in the database provide an effec-tive way of narrowing down the amount of images we have to process and select between. *(pic. 1)*

Nevertheless, if we look at the titles of the stripes, that have already been composed, it seems that it is often the aim to create a story, *(pic. 2)* pinpoint resemblance in motifs or oth-er more individual intentions, which are behind the selection. Thus, it seems that the database generates more than automat-ic stimuli responses from its users, and that it is in fact able to create a situation *(pic. 3)*, which at the same time as it high-lights the way in which technology may marginalise the effort-ful and deliberative aspects of thinking also manages to incite »the perceiver to discover relations between herself and as-pects of the environment.« The stripes produced by the users of the Signs of the City database seems proof that conscious at-tention is indeed generated, and the database succeeds in cre-ating a space for reflection on the contemporary modern Euro-pean metropolis.

This precarious position between attention and automatici-ty is also reflected in the way in which the theme of the project — signs of the city — has been approached. It can be argued that everyday life and the well-known places of our own city, which are the central focus points of the project, are in fact situated somewhere between automaticity and attention: most of what we see and do every day, becomes automatic occurrences to us, which we register without giving it special attention. Possi-bly more so in a large city, where the frequency of occurrences makes you pay less attention to events such as the siren of an ambulance or navigating through morning traffic on your bicy-cle. However, the fact that the young photographers have been asked to portray aspects of their everyday environment cre-ates a new type of awareness of the everyday. It is this con-scious awareness, in collaboration with digital cameras or mo-bile phones, which captures the signs of their city. The theme and execution of the project thus in its own way explore the

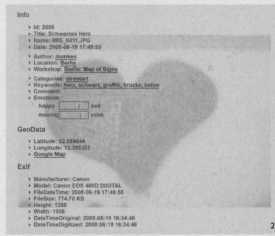

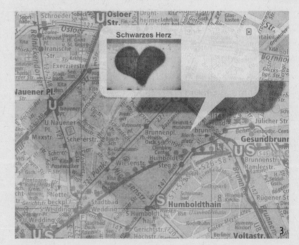

position of technology in generating attention in a familiar environment; and features such as GPS positioning help direct attention to issues, that might not otherwise have been noticed.

Again, we see an articulation of the delicate position of technology between generating space for creativity and controlling the same creativity.

The most powerful example of the way in which the Signs of the City database articulates the relation between city, technology, and attention can be observed in the individual image: when you have selected one image from the multitude, you are presented not only with the motif, its title, and keywords (all selected by the photographer), but also with the automatically (i.e., technically) generated data such as the camera details, image data, and GPS positioning. This may be regarded as a condensed articulation of the way in which Signs of the City embodies and discusses the intersection between an automatic technical registration of the surrounding world on the one hand, and on the other hand, an attentive reflection and focus, which is linked to the necessity of selection and the emphasis put on intentionality in the encounter with the city. It also highlights how essential and ubiquitous digital technology has been for this project, not only in the representation, but also in the production of the images.

The internet site of Lab for Culture highlights that Signs of the City shows »the impact of today's globally produced images and what kind of room for manoeuvre remains at the disposal of the individual.« This characteristic eloquently condenses the position of the project between automatism and attention — on the one hand an automatism supported by technology and our ability to create meaning, and on the other hand an exploration of the leeway for the individual in which there is room for conscious intention, organisation, and selection.

Signs of the City deals with two of the probably *most demanding* areas to which we can subject our sensory system: digital technology and the city. In the force field between these two it discusses the possibility that focussed conscious attention can arise. It does so, not by blocking out the flow of information surrounding it, nor by allowing technology in convergence with our »automatic machinery« to take control, but rather by making this negotiation part of its subject matter. Ironically, the database form (which is most often associated with the smooth management of massive data collections) seems especially well suited for this, because it can contain so much material. The database does not eliminate the noise and excessive flow of input that exists in a city, but draws it into the representation, making the navigation of the database resemble the experience of the contemporary cyber city. Hereby, it gives us important insight into the current condition of information processing, and also succeeds in creating a sign of the contemporary city, which provides space for hearing the voice of the metropolis without simplifying its complexity.

The Subjective Side of the Objective

Media Pedagogy looks at Signs of the City

by Prof. Dr. Franz Josef Röll, Darmstadt University of Applied Sciences

Media pedagogy deals with the social and cultural effects that information and communication technologies have on our society, our perceptions, and our culture of communication. Its role in relation to these effects is that of a critical companion in line with *Lebenswelt* (i.e., live-world) and action-oriented media pedagogical approaches to looking at urban environments. The Signs of the City project in Sofia related in particular to this approach. Young people came to terms with their social space by taking photographs. Strange spaces became familiar; they recognised the opportunities of their social space by looking at its image. Before I refer to the Signs of the City project, let me reflect on the difference between signs and symbols.

SIGNS AND SYMBOLS

Signs are a precondition of any form of culture and communication. They help us to find points of orientation in our world. On the one hand they can be read quite naturalistically, while on the other hand they carry conscribed meanings that become typified by cultural developments in history. Ongoing acceleration of social structures and changes in our perceptions also alter signage systems. It is never arbitrary to create a sign, it is ontological; subjects need to allocate meaning to a sign. Signs can be repeated in different contexts; however, they can also change their meaning in such repetitions. Nevertheless, stable connections can also be found between signs and meanings.

The sign function is composed of subject, sign, and object, whereas the symbol function is composed of subject, symbol, imagination, and object. Thus, the function of signification in relation to the subject marks the fundamental difference between sign and symbol.

The sign function is based on mutual understanding; the symbol adds the signification function to its informational function. Symbols can help to make the invisible and abstract visible and manifest.

They work metaphorically and, like discursive speech, they can bring new aspects into consciousness. The symbol or the symbolic performance is a comprehensive mode of communication, manifesting itself in different forms and changing in the process of manifestation. The human psyche itself can be understood as a process of symbolic transformation of psychophysical impulses.

MY CITY

The mode of taking photos of signs can rapidly charge the sign function with additional meaning. In the first example *(pic. 1)*, the sign »woman« has been sprayed onto the pavement with a stencil. It is photographed from a birds-eye perspective. This influences the subsequent viewer; likewise the selected frame (filling of the picture, omission of horizon) and the position of the sign in the picture frame, right from the centre. The monochrome grey of the background of the sign and the cracks in the pavement that divide the picture into five parts also add new meaning to it.

The youths' photos always carry information about the photographers. This is the subjective side of the objective of the camera. Even the photographic depiction of a sign is a constructive process of a subject. You can also draw hypotheses on the way and means that the photographer visually constructs reality from a picture of a sign. Photographers and subsequent viewers share the influences of four signage systems: a phylogenetic system of signs, a sociocultural system of signs, a generation-specific system of signs (*Zeitgeist*), and a biographic system of signs.

These four sources influence the development of a perception script; a blueprint for the individual construction of world images. Photographers need an active imagination to open up their source of inner pictures. By active imagination one understands the process of becoming aware of one's perception script. The database of photos in Signs of the City provides plenty of opportunities to decode these inner scripts.

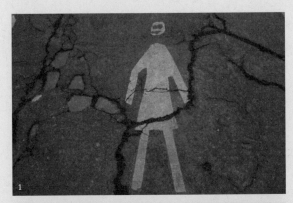

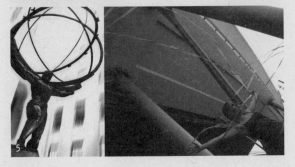

The mode of perception of individuals can be irritated by perturbations. Such perturbations are usually triggered by artists and peers within this project. Additionally, a place, a neighbourhood, a street, a building, or a room can inspire the awareness of things that have remained hidden so far.

Significantly, many photos use montage to comment on the sign frame. For example, the integration of two motifs into one picture constructs a productive tension. When the viewer recognises this montage he or she also immediately intervenes in the sign frame. I call this kind of photography »composition of chance«. A certain sign frame is defined as the background (for example, the graffiti of a rat or a tag). Then the photographer waits until a person crosses the picture frame by chance. The shot is taken at a point that was fixed beforehand in the imagination of the photographer. *(pic. 2, 3)*

To work on certain motifs from different angles, multidimensional composition and the difference in the results of this process teaches young people to replace their universalistic interpretation patterns with a multitude of perspectives and options for action. Composition within space also bears new narrative contexts.

At the same time, social space is habitualised. This space provides the surface on which conscious and unconscious aspects of self interact. This can be understood and used as an expression of the search for identity. Often this is combined with a confrontation with inner pictures. There is always a citation of signs and symbols in intermediary discourse. How these sociocultural experiences (conscious or unconscious) have an impact on the works of the young photographers can be demonstrated in many pictures.

The results of the workshop by Diego Ferrari at the House of World Cultures specifically show that the concept of staging body signs in architectural spaces is heavily related to the imaginary template of media cultural history. Thus, the motif of a woman's legs pointing skywards has often been used before in advertising *(pic. 4, 5)*.

Another image also quotes an icon of modernity. The image of a young woman »caught« in colourful tapes and ribbons cites the famous sculpture of Prometheus that stands in front of the New York's Rockefeller Centre. Inner images arguably manifest themselves within suburban contexts, and at the same time take recourse to images and image cultures, which we are already familiar with from popular media discourse.

However, there are further indications in other pictures as to how sociocultural transfers may slip into our own forms of perception. Underwriting the photographs of young people, whose eyes or mouths are covered (in this case with vertical black stripes) is the age-old allegory of the *»Three Wise Monkeys«*: one of them does not see, another does not speak, and the third does not hear. This motif has been used widely in the history of the art, amongst others by contemporary artist Keith Haring. Furthermore, we notice that the photgraphs take up topics, which are particularly singnificant within the realm of adolescent young people, e.g., hair. One such image is especially noteworthy; it is a photograph of a young woman, whose hair is taped to a glass window. With her eyes closed and her mouth slightly open as if in expectation, she seems at first sight to be nude, as we only see her bare shoulders. In the left part of the image a shadow seems to indicate a man moving towards this young woman. The image processes the motif of Snow White, an old German image motif of a sleeping and possibly imprisoned woman, waiting to be saved by a hero. The closed doors reinforce this impression. As her loose hair symbolically expresses — considered an erotic message in many cultures — she is full of expectation.

Aesthetic learning

Projects such as Signs of the City offer various opportunities for aesthetic education. Aesthetic education refers to the acquisition of complex perceptive skills, with which one's personal and external life-worlds — the experiences, activities, and environments that form an individual life — may be interpreted. Skills, which also serve to organize, explicate, test, assimilate, structure, and form our experiences. At the heart of the concept of aesthetic learning is the aim to develop and articulate perceptive and action-oriented skills, which can also be deployed in concrete everyday life.

It also serves to playfully and joyfully dismantle the illusion that cognitive processes are a truthful and veritable form of perception, without however damaging the identity of the individual. Aesthetic experiences can lead us to a so-called »light bulb moment« : the sudden realization of fundamental connections and interrelations between elements. Surprising impressions can lead us to amend previously held presumptions about reality. Important structural elements of aesthetic experience are, for example, surprise and pleasure. We speak of a flow level, when action and consciousness merge and we lose our sense of time and self-awareness. Both experiences open up new points of access to cognition. This exploratory function of aesthetic experience can also bring about a more fulfilled present. Aesthetic learning contributes to self-empowerment, enables us to develop new perspectives, overcome blockades in learning, reveals our own resources, and enables us to understand ourselves as a project and process. Above all, however, it encourages a visual form of dialogue with other perspectives, and thus supports intercultural communication.

Impressions from the Conference

by Andrew McIllroy, Freelance author, Brussels

The city escapes us. We live in it and yet are lived by it. Ourselves, these fragile bags of identity, are forced daily to negotiate an environment that is neither quite ours, nor quite alien to us. We construct it – obviously – and then it constructs us. In the city, it seems that we are constantly navigating risk, danger and excitement back to our small islands of warmth, safety, and regularity, which we then leave again, as if setting sail to new experiences and realities. This dilemma, this »seesaw« of experience, is what makes the city a perpetual process of growing up, an ever-refreshed journey through childhood and adolescent into adulthood. Ben Jonson famously said of London »When a man is tired of London, he is tired of life« and although the statement reeks of urban self satisfaction, it sums up the sense that to travel through the city is to travel through life itself.

That is why the youth view of the city is so important, and also why it is also so rare. Youth is in such a constant forward movement, forever throwing up new buildings and even building pathways, testing routes and venturing out unto rickety and perhaps unsafe bridges. Youth is in such turmoil of experimentation that it doesn't often have the time or the desire to review critique and apportion credit. When the young person talks to the city, he/she does so in a permanent engagement with its values and structures. The younger you are the more likely you are to demand that the city »come to you« and »fulfil you.« The older you are, the more you realise that the city is both aggressive and passive. The city »comes« to no one, it offers us nothing, it exists to be taken, to be used up, to be undermined and then to be rebuilt. The adult looks at the city and sees only scope for improvement. The young person looks at it and tries to understand what thing it is and how to navigate through it. The city for the adult is a place of exhaustion and for the young a place of energy.

Signs of the City is a testament to that energy. It exhausts me just looking at it! The whole project is a testament to the rejuvenating power of the city, and its youth, and its artists, to tell us stories. It acts as a witness to the urban fabric's potential to explain us to ourselves, to give us shape as social beings. The project and the outputs remind us that, just like the country *child* in some mythical nineteenth century idyll knew how to read the signs of weather, of bird call and of animal tracks, the twenty-first century *child* learns to read the city in an equally unique and sensitive way. And through that process of reading they also read their own identity. The challenge for us City Readers – that's you, reading this right now, unless you still live in a forest – is that the signs are shifting, multiform, and uncertain. Nothing means only one thing in the city; there is as much scope for interpretation in an urban road as there is in a forest – and perhaps as much danger and uncertainty, as much beauty, opportunity, and discovery. A car, for example, is both danger and freedom, an abandoned house speaks simultaneously of failure and renewal, a skate park is all at once fun and threatening, an office block coexists as oppressive marker and a call to adult independence, a palace is set of a double images – one for the tourist with a camera and one for the homeless guy on the corner.

During the conference in Berlin, reference was occasionally made to the failure of the website to cohere around one or two key logical principles, as if the core aim of the Signs of the City was somehow to come up with a neatly bound folder of policy implications and future planning strategies (either for the city, for youth, or for culture in general). In fact, the very chaos, profusion, and joy of the website speaks of the shapeless energy that is the city experience today and also, as an aside, of its potential to be excavated and interpreted. Of course, Signs of the City must move in the direction of analysis and synthesis. It must try to extract from image and experience something that is formal and precise. The work of the critic and the policy maker is always to highlight, discard, compare, and extrapolate from one thing to another and then to apply the abstractions to various fields of endeavour – to education or to city planning, to youth policy or to arts funding, to immigration debates or to creative industry and training frameworks.

The institutional framework around Signs of the City must rapidly move to formalise some concepts, some principles of what we might call »Urban Literacy« which may in time come to be seen as vital and important as »Citizenship« or »Intercultural Dialogue« and other Capital Letter Terms of Art. Who knows, perhaps urban literacy could become the animal husbandry of the future, a tool kit of skills, attitudes, and sensitivities that all young people will learn how to acquire to help them manage the urban experience. A degree of formalisation is urgent of course. We are a species whose habitat is both old (man has lived in cities since the start of civilisation) and new (we are psychically and psychologically at heart still hunters on the open savannah – if you don't believe me look at the shoppers in the Christmas sales!). What is more, it is in constant evolution. Never has man lived in such a multiform, socially shifting, and physically unpredictable setting. When we add the pressures of our civilisational zenith – mobility, ecological degradation, social inequality, education, media saturation, and community fragmentation – we see why the city eats into our capacity to respond meaningfully. The escape routes of cocooning (the outside does not exist), destruction (the outside can be made to disappear), or submission (the out-side overpowers and destroys me) are all only sporadically available. We have to engage with the city. Actively.

Signs of the City tells us something about that engagement but I wonder, looking at the website after the conference, and trying to remain open to it – in the same way as I might remain open to a work of art, to a poem, to a piece of architecture – if we are patient enough to read it? Men have a great drive towards rationalising and, while I stampede along with the others. I wonder if sometimes it isn't better just to look, experience and imagine? This slower *reading* of both the conference and the website cast up a series of words, anchor points, and ideas that pushed me into small conversation with myself about the city, the project, and the way we relate to youth in the city and I want to share these with you. This has no scientific content, it is all value-laden and personal, but the very one-offness may be valuable in other ways to the people who come along later and try to read the project as a whole. Maybe something will stick.

ANXIETY

The city speaks to us of anxiety, of the fear of being lost in the urban experience, of its uncontrollability, of what, Eric Corbijn, the Brussels based urban geographer, calls the »overwhelming city.« In most of the professional dialogues about the urban experience, it is seen as a challenge and problem, and the conference itself occasionally veered towards a language of »youth engagement« that reflects our adult preoccupations with youth as a vector for insecurity and doubt.

But the conference and the website, are actually oddly optimistic experiences. Both of these jigsaw pieces speak about the journey towards »making sense« in Alison Rooke's memorable phrase. And they reassured me that it is possible to feel good in the city, even thought this journey towards comfort is necessarily complex and uncertain. Velislava Donkin from Sofia spoke movingly about the psychological underpinning of the work that they did with their young people and underlined for me both the sense of curiosity that the young have towards the city, their emergent skills and confidence in dealing with it (sometimes to their own surprise), and of course their own language of sense and meaning that the pictures partially translate.

So, if anything, the project undermines anxiety as a condition of urban living. The prolific nature of the website – with its madcap rush of colour and form – makes a statement both about the uncontrollability of the city and the dogged, engaged enthusiasm to make sense of it anyway. The project has more formal art value than I suspected when I first came across the pictures on the web but again, the whole is about process, not product. The fact that the technical output reached impressive heights (and made it increasingly difficult to distinguish amateur from professional visions) was only an added artistic bonus.

Soul

It does something so odd that critics and enthusiasts are always reduced to purple prose, to emotional ambiguity when describing it. Art uncovers soul. Whatever it is that *art* does it isn't very amenable to language, nor description. But there is art in the project and this creative core to the work is vital in how it succeeds in representing the city as a place with soul. In our post-modern, post-visual, media-suffocated world the project acted as a call for attention. At its most basic it says »*Look at this; we found this interesting; we found this to have some meaning*.« The American artist Philip Guston said just before his death (with one likes to imagine in a tone of aggrieved surprise), »*... there is no substitute for the concrete*.« The phrase is radical, the more you linger on it. He wasn't just saying that the concrete is what we can have, but also I think that it is all we need to work with. The city, so much of a locus of imagination and abstract utopianism, is of course only a concrete, tangible, lived set of buildings and crossroads. Many architects and planners seem to spend their time submerged in a CGI heaven where the city becomes so many virtual ideals, so many possible / impossible images of utopian living that one wonders if they ever walk down a street, or go to a kebab stand. Signs of the City offers the viewer a dizzying selection of concrete narratives of the young person's city. This concrete effusion is of course both terrifying and also exciting I say *narrative* but in fact the images as presented are rather more like a vocabulary, they lack a grammar or syntax; you might even cruelly say they lack style. That is perhaps the next step – the imposition of order or orders on a mass of spiky material. That isn't their job, the people who took these photos; their job was just to look. The slower, more reflective amongst us need to construe.

Story

We all construe stories in our own way. Some people will see a story of urban chaos, and some of volcanic aesthetic resources. Some will see the small friendships and personal turnings that the processes caused, and some others will see the looming urban challenges that each young person has inadvertently captured (I am certain, absolutely certain, that no one who took part did so in the sense of trying to diagnose what was wrong with their city: they may have come out of it with anecdotes about their city and a sense of what might be done better, but these photos do not, to me anyway, tell a story of despair for the city). This story I see / hear is one of emergent citizenship. Someone in the conference memorably spoke of the »easyJet nation« in reference to the post-1980 generation, who either travel or if they don't have access to images from all over the world and are thus inured or dulled to the impact of other cultures. But the project also suggests to me that even our battle hardened urban youth are still fresh and innocent and that a new experience (the first olive, hearing a foreign language, learning to use a camera) can alert the DNA of the soul in a totally unpredictable way. The story (yours, mine, the city's) has to start somewhere, after all, and in Signs of the City the story starts with the creative energy, the participation, and the willingness of the participants to explore. All this inchoate substance has yet to be shaped, but everything (even the European project) has a first step.

Danger

A certain danger lies within the project and it is the one that Susan Sonntag was fond of referring to when she talked about the »democracy of images« that we live through. She wasn't sure that it was a totally good thing. She worried that too many pictures robs us of our capacity to distinguish and to judge, that they dull our moral sense; after all, one dead baby in picture is very much like another. In our mediated world (I read somewhere that three or four or twelve billion images are taken every day, the exact figure is so huge its precision is no longer of any importance) we risk being submerged by demagoguery of images, a kind of tyranny of the visual. Several artists have tried to work with this – most notably for example the Delete! project by artists Christoph Steinbrener and Rainer Dempf who covered all street signs in Vienna with huge yellow tarpaulins to »clean up« and »refresh« the city landscape. The result was alien and disturbing and hugely successful. Cities like Sao Paolo have become advertising free cities in an attempt to reclaim the visual field, to liberate it if you like. Of course, we all do this in our own little way every day. We select and edit. But the project made me think that there is no way to understand the city as a visual story anymore, that it is beyond my skills and probably anyone's skills to explain. T.S. Eliot posed the question: »Where is the wisdom we have lost in knowledge? Where is the knowledge we have lost in information?« The Signs project is like a visual helter skelter of that statement. Who will make sense of it for us? Institutions and funders expect someone to – that is where they are at their most comfortable. Linear thought is what they like and the project does seem to have delivered a lot of it – the speakers at the conference in particular were admirably good at synthesising what the project might mean or how it might evolve.

Such rationalising, so important in terms of evaluation, can sometimes blind us to the real potential for wisdom, because that is often not amenable to measurement. Sonntag, a great rationalist, would probably want to argue for the need to interpret anyway. The project, workshops, training, and exhibitions, the website and its mass of playful material, as well as the conferences and studies are all part of what we might call an Edison Laboratory (Edison had a huge room filled with rubbish and objects of all kinds that people were invited to come and play with and assemble or explore ideas on the basis of putting things together). The Signs project is like the laboratory before many people have started to assemble stuff.

That's the next step coming up, the step that leads to connecting. The connections are amongst ourselves, with specialists and policy makers, with teachers and planners and governments, and finally across Europe, We should not worry that the connections themselves are chaotic and unpredictable.

We are too linear in our expectations. The struggle for citizenship is itself a lumpy affair. The citizen is the stranger in the city, the face you do not know but accept nevertheless.

Faces

Why did I jump to the word citizenship? Quite a leap of logic someone will say. Well, not, really. The Signs project is about relationships. A lot of the language round the conference underlined for me that the words we were using – terms such as *Zeichen* (sign) or *Dialog* or *Seele* (soul) – are just short-hand for people doing things together. Sometimes this was learning, sometimes collaborating, sometimes doing, sometimes talking, sometimes meeting, and sometimes exhibiting. The exhibitions above all reflect the face-to-face nurture of the experience, the lived encounter. They demonstrate *Zugehörigkeit* (belonging, also a term much used over two days) and the narrative of belonging means to belong somewhere or to someone. The artists themselves gave huge amounts of time, energy, interest, and commitment to sharing their individuality with these young people so that they to might learn a language of sharing, of commonality. Art is very selfish but also very generous. Artists are egotists also do it for the whole world. They are not a bad model of the conflict we all face, which may explain why everyone is an artist now, everyone is seeking to share their uniqueness with the mass of mankind. It is one of the powers of the artist to meld the individual with the shared through the work of art and not to default into violence. Artists are often not very nice people but we have to admit they seldom start wars. Interestingly, there is a creative tension with the balancing desires for individualism and belonging – neither I nor anyone over the age of thirty will probably live to see how the twenty-first century finds a balance between those two opposing demands. All we can hope is that we do it better than the nineteenth or the twentieth, for nationalism, totalitarianism, Marxism, and capitalism areall attempts to find a way to bind the individual to the group – which is why they are all utopian, counter-intuitive as that may seem – and none of them have really come up with the goods. Citizenship lies for me at the very heart of the European experience and we have had lots of time to explore it, from Greek through Renaissance models, to Enlightenment and Industrial versions, to today's connectivity and technology as the corner stones. But we haven't decided what it means, neither for the locality, the national state nor the European project.

We are entering into a new paradigm of dialogue and exchange, marked by interculturalism and by globalism. The pictures on the web site tell that story, too: the story of who we are in the city and who we might become.

Change

Is it an optimistic project? Joseph Stieglitz, the Nobel Economist says that when you see the light at the end of the tunnel you ought to remember it might be a train coming straight at you! Jolly. I am cheered up by the project but also ask myself how to rise to the challenges it poses. How did it impact on participants, on the artists, on the policy makers? How does the city impact on the individual? Susanne Stemmler said at the opening session of the conference that »these signs invite a response« and that is the problem. I have no response that isn't about more questions. What kind of city? What kind of community do I have right now, and what kind do I want to build? How can I connect to youth? (What do we do to join up the energy of one with the reflection of the other? It's the old, old question of time, that silent traitor. *Si la joventud supiera, si la vejez pudiera*, say the Spanish – if age could and youth knew. One of my favourite poets, Susan Oldes talks about poetry as »an attempt to swim upstream against the current of time,« and while not getting too purple in my prose, that seems as good a slogan for the project as anything. No sooner taken, these images are already old. No sooner captured, but they are out of date. No sooner young and open, but the participants will move into age and experience.

The malleable will become fixed. The possible will be probable. And yet what we need is change. This is what we believe in. All the European projects, trasnfrontier explorations, and intercultural dialogue I have witnessed or heard about in Europe over the last ten years have had one common theme: we believe in change; we believe we can mould the future. Not as dictators, or demagogues, but as players. It is the story of vision, or rather a mosaic of images, a scatter of pictures, which come together and make up a vision of what is possible. Suddenly the Signs of the City project seems to mean something else to me, something that only photography can communicate. I look again through the site. Brassaï's *The Riviera* came to mind while looking at some of the images, and in particular one of two boys in Barcelona leaping after a ball, a picture that seems to glow with its own inner light. In Brassaï's photo a man sits by the sea, under an umbrella, on a bench. The umbrella is huge and white and it glows. It is less that light falls on it than the light streams out of it. It is a visionary image, precisely because all the meaning, all the light, all the intensity comes out from that umbrella. The image means nothing – it has no syntax of sense – but it communicates a huge, impossible importance. It says: »... this object is profoundly mysterious you know, this object contains its own story ... « The boys playing football do the same thing for me – they are visionary, they show the city in action but explain nothing, they tell the story of their own childish energy and relate it to no one. The picture, with its warm glow of the setting sun and its odd mixture of urban decay and youthful excitement, momentarily makes everything, anything, possible. It is a joyous image. It is the city, not in some rose tinted tourism spectacle. It is the city as lived, not as imagined, and it is, quite frankly, beautiful.

Earlier I mentioned image and experience. The act of photography is of course both; both a fixed image and the memory of the experienced moment. The project, as all art projects, shares this tension between the static and the fluid. Art is in fact the paralysed creative moment, the singularity that the artist creates out of all the energy at her disposal. Art says »I lived this and then I stopped it here.« When the young people who produced this work were creating, they themselves were plunged into the middle of experience.

While I have no doubt that the longerterm value of the project lies in the theorising, semiotics, anthropology, architecture and sociology, that it will give rise to, I leave those languages to other people for I do not manipulate them well. But the immediate value of the project lies in what the teams, young people, and artists did together, and how they learned to do it and what they might even decide to do next. It is less that the project is necessarily a transformative one, but more that it opens the door to individual awareness of transformation.

This attentive opening of doors, this shining of light on the youth experience in the city now requires our energy to decode it. Just not too soon. The project vibrates with the fissile electricity of youth and optimism and may even shake open some doors, expose some cracks in our understanding of how we read youth and the city. Signs of the City gives us an *option* of urbanity (in both senses of the term urbanity).

And alongside this option lies another, the *option* of European identity (in the hundreds of senses of the term European). These options are open, negotiable, still a bit unformed, and floppy. But they do exist and we fail to celebrate them enough. They are germinating in the city alongside other, ranker, less attractive growths. When we look at the city we tend to see the *mauvaise herbe*, the weeds, nettles, and the thorns. Sometimes we should stop looking for the negative. Sometimes, in fact, we are too clever for our own good. Signs of the City is a sharp little knock that reminds us to look up from our paper, over our coffee cup, down and off to one side, to see through the fence, to have an oblique and sideways glance at the street corner, to peer *over there*, beyond the railway track, under the gas canister and on top of the window ledge and recognise that there are lots of oddities flourishing in our city. The project asks us all to be young. And look.

Evaluation

chapter six

Project Evaluation

Dr. Alison Rooke,
Centre for Urban and Community Research,
Goldsmiths College, University of London

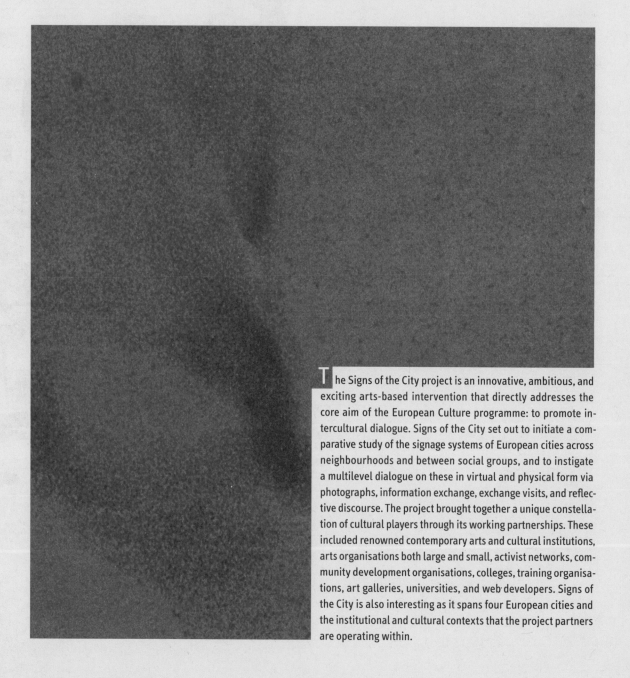

The Signs of the City project is an innovative, ambitious, and exciting arts-based intervention that directly addresses the core aim of the European Culture programme: to promote intercultural dialogue. Signs of the City set out to initiate a comparative study of the signage systems of European cities across neighbourhoods and between social groups, and to instigate a multilevel dialogue on these in virtual and physical form via photographs, information exchange, exchange visits, and reflective discourse. The project brought together a unique constellation of cultural players through its working partnerships. These included renowned contemporary arts and cultural institutions, arts organisations both large and small, activist networks, community development organisations, colleges, training organisations, art galleries, universities, and web developers. Signs of the City is also interesting as it spans four European cities and the institutional and cultural contexts that the project partners are operating within.

The Signs of the City project has been evaluated by the Centre for Urban and Community Research (CUCR) Goldsmiths, University of London. CUCR develops work that is both rooted in contemporary debates and in urban social theory. CUCR is committed to an ethical engagement with contemporary city life. The Centre's teaching and research work is concerned with the role of the arts and creative industries in urban change, urban governance, as well as developing multimedia research and evaluation methodologies. In this sense, the ethos of work at the Centre has been informed by an aspiration to combine a Frankfurt School commitment to critical reflection with a Chicago School commitment to empirically informed social research. Apart from evaluating Signs of the City, CUCR has also been an academic partner to the project, providing a sociological perspective on the project's development and on the significance of the overall project. While space does not allow for a detailed discussion of the project's successes and challenges city by city, we would like to address the challenges that evaluating such an undertaking poses and to discuss some of the project's significant features.

Signs of the City represents an interesting and creative approach to investigating the EU Culture programme's central aspiration to a foreground role for culture in understanding European citizenship as set out clearly here:

> »It is essential to promote cooperation and cultural exchanges in order to respect and promote the diversity of cultures and languages in Europe and improve knowledge among European citizens of European cultures other than their own, while at the same time heightening their awareness of the common European cultural heritage they share. [This, it is stated,] helps to make European citizenship a tangible reality by encouraging direct participation by European citizens in the integration process.« Decision No 1855/2006/EC of the European Parliament and of the Council of 12 December 2006 establishing the Culture Programme (2007 to 2013)

The question of the role of culture in promoting a tangible understanding and awareness of Europeanness is central to the

Signs of the City project in its use of visual and creative methodologies to investigate young people's rights to the European cities in which they live; whether this be at the level of neighbourhood, metropolis or beyond. It is significant that much of the project takes place during the European Year of Intercultural Dialogue, which seeks to help raise the awareness of all those living in the EU, especially young people, of the importance of engaging in intercultural dialogue in their daily lives and of becoming active European citizens. Within the EU culture programme, one of these objectives is to »strengthen respect for cultural diversity and deal with the complex reality in our societies and the coexistence of different cultural identities and beliefs.« It also specifically addresses non-citizens and those living temporarily in the EU. The project converts the meta-narratives of Europeanness into encounters – whether on or offline, visual or tangible – which cross the boundaries of nation-states and the complex identities that exist within them.

EVALUATING SIGNS OF THE CITY

The objective of the Signs of the City evaluation was to analyse and discuss the project's key elements, its process and success, as well to oversee the overall quality management of the project. The ethos of the evaluation was participatory in that it ran alongside the delivery of the project, offering the various partners and stakeholders an opportunity to reflect on the project's successes, challenges, and wider significance; in order to overcome the practical barriers of space and time. However, evaluating a large network that is spread across four European cities with this ethos creates considerable logistical challenges.

At the outset of the project, it was planned to use an evaluation toolkit (a set of evaluation tools to ensure that each city team collect and summarise data) for use by the individuals in each city who took primary responsibility for the evaluation. The idea was that each of the artists delivering the workshop would use the tools to reflect on the workshop and record matters of significance. However, this original plan was amended in February 2008. Changes to the project delivery, and the various timescales of delivery resulted in alterations in the structure of the evaluation work programme. In addition, while the evaluation tools provided a set of flexible resources that artists and partners could potentially use to appraise the impact of their practice, the variety of artistic approaches to the workshops and the availability of artists to conduct evaluation within the time constraints of the workshop presented considerable difficulties. Furthermore, the fact that costs of living and fees for educators and artists varied substantially across the participating cities meant that the intensity and length of engagement of the young people could not be consistent across the workshops. The same amount of money was most effective in Sofia, whereas it could only pay for less extensive engagement between artists and young people in London. It became apparent that a »one size fits all« approach to evaluation was not appropriate. It was therefore altered from one comparing the projects in each city to considering the themes that were common to the variety of workshops, and the learning from the specific models employed.

LOCAL CONTEXTS, EUROPEAN VISIONS

The rich variety of approaches to the workshops reflect individual artistic methodologies, which in turn reflect various regional and national contexts of participatory arts and community development, as well as the local histories of artistic practitioners and funding institutions in the four participating cities. It was both a strength and a challenge of the project that these varied significantly across the locations of the project. A review of the work of the project partners illustrates both their similarities and differences; for example, there is a more established framework for arts funding and a recognition of the role of the cultural industries in structuring economic change in a city in Barcelona, Berlin, and London, while this is not the case in Sofia.

In Barcelona, community arts is a relatively new term, which it has been argued, has been appropriated by cultural policies in an attempt to stimulate national funding (in part inspired by the UK Arts Council model). In this context, there is no consistent policy for the development, evaluation or recognition of community arts. In addition, there is a considerable institutional split between »high art« galleries and community arts, although occasionally important cultural or art centres may develop a sudden and brief interest in carrying out art projects in conjunction with a community or school. In recent times the cultural sector has shown a renewed interest in community arts and in developing collaborations with communities or »non-artists.« The Barcelona Signs of the City workshops to

some extent reflect this division, while simultaneously providing a significant opportunity for experimentation and future collaborations that span these sectoral divides in that it brings together a network of community organisations and a large professional artistic production centre and their varied social and cultural capitals. The workshops were delivered with a strong commitment to reaching young people who can be described as socially excluded or disadvantaged as a result of their economic situations, immigration status, or location. Traditions of civic activism are perhaps strongest in Barcelona, where the arrival of democracy is still within living memory of many arts educators. This spirit is reflected in the delivery of the Barcelona workshops, which were facilitated through an established network of social support centres and neighbourhood projects within a strong local culture of civic activism. Their focus was, in general, one of participatory photography, skilfully reaching young people from diverse and excluded groups using straightforward photographic technologies to document their social realities. These workshops reflected a strong community development ethos, aiming to bring young people together and involve them in the network of centres and services, wider opportunities for democratic participation, and positive activities.

Traces of the the divisions of east and west that predated the fall of the wall remain to be seen in Berlin, although arts-led gentrification is proceeding apace in the eastern parts of the city. The workshops there were delivered with particularly strong and imaginative artistic concepts. This is to some extent a reflection of the primary partner's networks and the presence of international artists in a city in which arts-led gentrification is flourishing. In addition, the Berlin partnership's involvement of education, employment, and training organisations has led to a degree of reflection and learning in regard to the value of participatory photography, less orthodox pedagogical styles, and the ways in which the transferability of these skills and approaches might be incorporated into existing training programmes.

There is no existing tradition of community or participatory arts or youth work in Sofia. There the workshops combined an artistic approach to photography (focussing on technical skills and aesthetics) with a commitment to providing a valuable and exceptional space for self-reflection and exploration of young Bulgarian people's identities in the context of rapidly developing urbanism.

The London workshops were delivered by four partners who belong to a funded and recognised arts sector that provides space for professional artists and programmes of participatory and community arts. There is a well-developed tradition of community arts and community development in this city. This is reflected in the range of partners who provided an infrastructure for the project, including space, participants, artists, and expertise in working with a range of interactive technologies. The workshops ranged from a traditional participatory photographic approach to more experimental ones using mobile and GPS technologies. Furthermore, urban regeneration and community development programmes involving matters such as health, safety, and cohesion have recently resulted in the popularity of participatory and community arts to meet these programme's aims. To some extent this reflects the city's recognition of the significance of cultural industries for its economy.

Reading the Visual

One of the central aims of the Signs of the City project was to develop a set of workshops, in collaboration with artists, which would explore how young people read the »signs of their cities,« to create an opportunity for young people to develop a visual inventory of the city, and to develop their visual literacy. In accordance with these aims, the Citipix website offers an important forum in which the participating young people can select photographs and upload them in order to share them with other participants and artists taking part in the project as well as the wider public. In this way, the Citipix image bank provides a distinct visual account of the four European cities. The Citipix platform was specifically designed to prioritise visual expression and dialogue, thus bypassing some of the more problem-

atic and potentially expensive issues of translation into four languages. The platform allowed the participants to share and use each other's photographs, also giving them the opportunity to visually explore European cities.

The Citipix web platform provides clear evidence of the participants' visual expression of themselves, and their production of genuinely interesting photographs; one of the challenges that evaluating the Signs of the City project presented was to make sense of those photographs. Another specific challenge was to assess the sociological significance of the photographs in order to evaluate the extent to which they, and the conditions of their production and circulation met the aims and objectives of the project. This led to broader questions of the extent to which

sociological and cultural argument can be made beyond the written word and how the photographs produced could be read. The individual workshops took place in each city using the technological means available. Apart from their one similarity that they have been taken by young people in European cities, it cannot be assumed that the photographs have any other underlying commonality, due to several factors including, the diversity of the participants themselves. So for example, the definition of the category »young people« varies across the cities. In Berlin this extended to people as old as thirty. In other cities workshops included participants as young as nine. In addition, the participants' visual competencies vary enormously. Some school children had never had the chance to hold a camera before. Others were arts students or amateur photographers with considerable experience of the discipline. This meant that participants came to the workshops with a wide range of technical and creative skills. Furthermore, they had access to different levels of technology (digital SLR cameras, mobile phone cameras, 35 mm film cameras, low-tech »point and shoot« digital cameras, pinhole cameras made of cardboard boxes). As a result some participants were able to produce photographs with a great deal of creative control and consideration of aesthetics. Others worked in more documentary fashion. These factors prevented any straightforward comparative reading of the large number of photographs produced in the four cities. They also led to a range of readings of the photographs uploaded onto the Citipix web platform. The photographs can be understood as an individual participant's signs of *their* city and their personal resonances (and therefore there is a relationship between the photographs produced by an individual); as collective readings of the city reflecting collective decisions about which photographs the participants wanted to upload as a *group* based on their merit in relation to the workshop themes (and therefore there is a relationship between the photographs uploaded in the session); as attempts to adhere to an artist's brief for the workshops; and finally as evidence of an understanding of photographic genres, technical and aesthetic merit. Therefore, when examining the Citipix platform the question becomes one of whether the meanings of the groups of photographs are internal to the groups' uploading criteria, the city workshops, or even across the cities.

BETWEEN SEMIOTICS AND YOUTH GEOGRAPHIES?
»THE CITY IS OUR COMPASS«

The evaluation of the Signs of the City project also leads to some interesting questions raised by the project's methodology; specifically how might we make sense of the photographs uploaded onto the web platform, when the diverse approaches of the artists reflected varied degrees of interest in social relations outside its framework? One of the challenges was to find a way of making sense of the uploaded photographs when as evaluators we could attend all of the sessions at which the photographs were discussed. We thus had to rely on the artists and evaluation leaders to communicate to us the *meaning* and *significance* of the photographs and what they articulate in relation to the aims of the project and workshop. (This was one of the main focuses of evaluation visits to the participating cities.) In some cases the photographs may be considered merely records or data, with few aesthetic merits but considerable symbolic significance, while others have more aesthetic merit but less significance in terms of what they are signs of (i.e., the social relations outside of the frame). In interpreting these photographs we can employ a semiotic reading of the photographs, i.e., the photographs are »signs« of the European city. In taking the photographs, the young people produced signs of their cities, which can be read as indications of how they comprehend the visual cultures of the city. Some of the workshops were delivered by artists who employed a literal interpretation of the term signs, i.e., taking photographs of the various sign systems of their city, employing GPS technologies to map these subjective impressions onto the official empirical representations of the city. Others entered into a discussion of semiotics; i.e., What is a sign? Is it an infrastructure for the framework? What is an image a sign of? How can we use photography to produce signs? These questions are of particular significance as far as the European aspects of the project are concerned. A sign (whether a »street sign« or a significant building) may have a clear meaning *within* a city but this may not be easily read without the associated local cultural understandings. There may also be specific local interpretations of semiotics. Clearly photographs have slippery meanings.

A sociological approach to the photographs reads them as indications of *how* young people inhabit the space of the city, navigate its risks, play in its public spaces, commemorate its pasts, and imagine its futures. Here the photographs have broader sociological meanings. The challenge, in terms of evaluation, has been one of understanding the meaning of the image both within and beyond the framework. Such consideration of the photographs points towards the significance of the project *process* (the participatory workshops and exchange visits and their impact on the participants) as much as its *product*

(the web platform). The uploaded photographs show us young people's experience of their neighbourhoods, the significance of certain places, and the journeys young people have taken as a part of the project. For example, in Barcelona the young people from Roquetas took a trip to the beach and put themselves into the picture – of the city – as a group. This was the first time they had made this short, but significant trip. Homeless young men in London explored parts of the city that they were usually prohibited from lingering in. In Barcelona, young migrant children went out into the streets with expensive cameras disrupting local shopkeepers' negative preconceptions of this group. In Berlin, young people returned to places that were significant when they were children, reliving journeys and crossing boundaries between east and west that are no longer physically apparent. Clearly the photographs produced here are so much more than signs or a »visual inventory« of the city. They are evidence of moments, spatial interventions, and temporary disruptions to some of the narrower definitions of what it is to be a citizen in a European city.

ARTISTIC PRACTICES

One of the strengths of the Signs of the City workshops is the way that they have employed so many methodologies that are beyond traditional participatory photographic practice, which most often involves giving participants low-tech cameras to document an aspect of their social lives under the guidance of an artist or development worker, sometimes followed up by photo elicitation interviews. Many of the Signs of the City workshops went beyond this straightforward approach. The workshops included approaches that are imaginative, performative, playful, archaeological, and experimental. At times the act of taking photographs in public was itself a spatial intervention.

In the workshop run by Diego Ferrari at the House of World Cultures in Berlin, the participants adopted a conceptual approach to photography by constructing their own signs – by, for example, introducing an object into a space or performing a small happening, thus learning how to change the dynamics and the meaning of the space through these interventions.

The workshop run by Cambellworks reveals some of the pedagogical potentials of photography. The workshop ran over a week with a group of young people who were either deaf or whose hearing was impared. In this workshop participants learned the principles of pinhole technology, built their own cameras, helped to build a mobile dark room, produced negatives that they used to create multilayered positive photographs, and uploaded them on to a web platform. Apart from moving through the history of photograpy in five days, young people were able to experiment with an alternative mode of expression to the written or spoken (rather signed) language throughout the workshop.

The workshop led by Martin Ruge at OSZ KIM, Berlin, explored and documented the signage system of the city using GPS technology and digital cameras. Digital photographs were allocated to their places of origination via GPS data in a geo-tagging process and uploaded onto an interactive online-map of Berlin. The city can be read through its signs using this map. Martin's workshop is an example of how the concepts central to the project, exploring the signage systems of the European city, can be interrogated and worked within a vocational training concept, bringing together artistic practice, technology, and graphic design.

Developing the Skills of Young People.

The limits of the evaluation timescale and the challenges of geography do not allow for a study of the project's broader impact. Many of the participants »came and went« in the cities in which the project was delivered through short-term, one-off or in very brief workshops. Some have shown more long-term interest and have returned to become involved in helping out in workshops, curating exhibitions and attending conferences. However, the five categories below summarise the main impact of the workshops on their participants

- **Craft Skills:** improved arts and craft skills e.g., photography, GPS, IT and digital media skills
- **Creative Skills:** experimentation, story-telling, imagination, reflection, expression, creating pieces of work, developing ideas, editing, curation
- **Life Skills:** communication, decision-making, personal development, organisational skills, sense of direction, motivation, successfully dealing with changes and challenges, teamwork, social development, time-keeping, confidence, self esteem
- **Media and Arts Inclusion:** diversity of participants engaged in arts practice, developing new pathways, working with professionals, networking, experiencing new events, places and spaces, increasing arts-based cultural and social capital
- **Employability:** organisational skills, planned and realistic aspirations/goals, networking, increased aspirations, initiative, teamwork, taking up opportunities, being ready for employment, good time-keeping, good self presentation, pursuing own projects, identifying next steps, and risk/enterprising behaviour

Urban Literacy

The project's impact on the participants has been realised in large and small, but no less significant, ways. For example, in working with disadvantaged young people in Barcelona and giving a young person a camera to hold and take away for a few days demonstrates a level of trust and respect not experienced by them before. In Berlin, a group of long-term unemployed people were successful in learning to work as a group and in curating and producing an exhibition of their work. This was a great success and was attended by over 150 people. However, another significant factor about the workshops is their demonstration of an interesting range of skills and modes of

learning. One of the main aims of the project was to investigate young people's experience of the European City, as an »arena« of intercultural encounter and a space in which identities are formed and moulded. It also aimed to sensitise participants and observers to the multiple layers of signs in urban landscapes and to encourage critical engagement with these often global signage systems. The evaluation bears witness to the ways in which participants combine photographic practice with their own previous experiences of city life. Participants have critically explored the visual cultures of European cities; they have read their cities as visual texts and have also creatively appropriated, translated, and reinterpreted the »signs of their cities.« The notion of »urban literacy« points towards some of the cultural competencies gained in the workshops as young people have learned to read the city, its image, and images in new ways by combining the visual and narrative elements of their senses of identity, belonging, and citizenship. This is evidenced in the ways that participants have produced their own signage systems by creatively editing visual landscapes to produce personal narratives of place, by excavating the existing signs of their city, by expanding their geographies through exploring new areas of the city, by following visual messages in the street leading to new interpersonal encounters, by exploring their rights to city spaces and the visual regulation of the city, by reflecting on communist and post-communist urbanism and the impact of global capitalism on the city landscape, and by developing an understanding of the logics of architectural space.

BETWEEN THE LOCAL LENS AND EUROPEAN VISIONS

Coordinating and delivering photographic workshops across four cities presents considerable challenges in terms of communication, logistics, conceptualisation, and evaluation. With this challenge in mind, »urban dialogues« designed the project with two events at the outset to bring together the project partners, the evaluation team, and the artists themselves; the kick-off meeting in Berlin and the Arts Education Lab. These events ensured that all attendees understood their roles and responsibilities within the Signs of the City network, that they understood the project aims and could locate their local work within the bigger European picture. They were also valuable opportunities for the project partners and artists to meet, to engage in productive dialogue, and to share their experience of arts and participatory practice across the political and cultural contexts of the four European settings. This European dimension of the project was attractive to many of the project partners as it represented an opportunity to be part of a European network of artists and arts organisations working in similar ways with similar groups of young people. As the following quotes illustrate:

> »Going to Berlin and meeting the other artists. I don't usually get to talk about this kind of work with artists in such depth, to think about the ideological basis of why we do this work and how we do it. I definitely think I have got links now with those artists and if I was in those cities I could go and see those artists. That was unexpected...« (Signs of the City Artist)

> »When you are running workshops you are really lost in the detail of it and also need to keep overview, so having those four days together really helped to keep the overview, of what it was for, what I was trying to achieve. And so you get to imagine what the workshop was like by looking at the rather impersonal website.« (Signs of the City Artist)

SEEING THE EUROPEAN

In the early stages of the project, evaluation visits and interviews revealed the extent to which many young people's minds work predominantly at the level of the habitual, the neighbourhood, and the local. In many cases artists found it challenging to get young people to reflect on their reading and experience of the city beyond the immediacy of the local. However, one common theme that did emerge involved the way in which participants were making sense of their city in terms of the global: taking photographs of places that resonate with their global connections. This was often due to matters of heritage and migration; it raised the question as to the extent to which

young people's minds work at the level of the European. Indeed »Europeaness« did not seem to feature explicitly in many of these photographs. While the photographs on the web platform are evidence of the visual landscape of European cities when viewed together and interacted with, without this interactivity it appeared that the European is hard to visualise and evidence visually for most participants. With this background, the LAB2 »Show me your City« event in October offered a valuable opportunity to explore the explicitly European aspects of the project more thoroughly.

The LAB2 exchange programme that took place from 6-10 October 2008 in Barcelona is, in many ways, at the heart of the Signs of the City project. It was a valuable and unique opportunity for a selection of participants from across the participating countries to meet face-to-face, to engage in inter-cultural dialogue, and to work collaboratively. It addresses the dimensions of the project that speak explicitly to the European culture programme's agenda i.e., encouraging intercultural dialogue and exploring the role of culture in engendering a sense of European citizenship amongst young people. A total of fifteen participants travelled to Barcelona to attend the LAB2 workshop; they were divided into three groups with five participants from each city. The range of ages between the groups was eleven years, the youngest participants being fourteen years old and the oldest twenty-five years old. In addition three artists (Nuria Calafell, Javier Oliden, and Paula Kleiman of Teleduca) from the Artibarri network facilitated contact with local Barcelona youth; approximately thirty young people from Barcelona attended the workshops. The young people participating in Barcelona were for the most part taking part in Signs of the City for the first time.

The exchange was instructive in understanding the ways in which being European is felt in different ways for the participants, all of whom came to the exchange from different starting points. One of the concepts, which underpins the idea of a European identity, is that of belonging to a nation-state which in turn belongs to Europe. The participants' own identities were diverse in terms of their heritage, so that for example the participants from London and Berlin included those which were British-African, British-Asian, British-Afro-Caribbean, and German-Turkish. The Barcelona participants included young people who were recent arrivals from the Philippines, North African, West Africa, Pakistan, as well as Roma young people. Some of these had no citizenship status. Many participants who had family ties to non-European countries had also travelled to their parents' country of origin which included: Nigeria, Somalia, Jamaica, Trinidad, India, Kenya, America, Dubai, the Philippines, and Turkey. High levels of travel can indicate a level of awareness and experience held by participants of foreign cultures and difference, and for many also shows developed understanding of other European countries and how a network of countries exists in relation to their home country. The notion of a group of young European citizens from each city with a homogenous national identity is not useful here. The languages and cultural understandings that were shared by the participants reflected global movements beyond a straightforward concept of Europeaness. So for example one of the artists, Javier Oliden, discussing a workshop with London and Barcelona young people stated:

»I think that from the kids I was working with, there was a guy from Congo who had been living in France and Switzerland, one from Ghana and three from the Philippines. So for them the question of the identity is western world and third world. [T]here is this conflict in the way that they feel a bit western and in another way they have their roots, and for them I think it is good to meet others and feel that they can communicate. So they have something that's the same.«

These connections of heritages and cultural experiences beyond Europe were explored in the encounters between the young people. In one workshop encounter a girl from London was asked to say her name. The Barcelona youth were having trouble pronouncing it at which point another participant who originated from Ghana realised that her name was Islamic. They went on to discover other shared similarities. In the same workshop, the Philippine participants were able to communicate with participants from England more easily than with Catalan or Spanish participants due to the fact that English is one of the official languages of the Philippines. So while a wide range of non-European national identities had some direct relevance to participants, the concept of European-ness was rather more abstract. At a workshop in Trinidat Vella, one local young woman who had lived all of her life in Barcelona asked the facilitator Nuria Calafell Obiol, »What's Europe?« She did not know whether England was part of Europe or the United States. While this is a small indicator of an increased interest in Europeanness, it also shows how the concept is somewhat removed from many young people's immediate concerns and awareness.

RECOGNISING THE HETEROGENEITY AND HOMOGENEITY OF EUROPEAN CULTURES

While the participants rarely discussed »Europeaness« per se, they did engage with Barcelona as a European city. Participants compared their experience of Barcelona and the experiences of participants from other cities with their own experience of living in their home city. An awareness of the global and European aspects of urban change was reflected in their photographic interests. The apparent ubiquity of the urban development of former industrial areas came up in discussions when participants from London and Sofia were taken on an Urban Space walk with Stefan Horn to the area Poble Nou. Many participants were unimpressed by the contemporary »glass and steel« architecture making comments such as »We have these in Sofia, I am going to the Museum« and »Yeah this is just like London« and »I really don't like that kind of thing, the modernistic buildings, we all have this stuff also and I get tired of seeing this.« Instead many participants were keen to seek out signs and sights that were unique to Barcelona. This was clearly an act of comparison. It was explored in an evaluation session in which participants were asked to show photographs that said something about what they had learned from Barcelona and specifically how the city compared with their home city and what their home city could learn from Barcelona. These presentations were revealing. The Sofia group were struck by many of the similarities between Barcelona and Sofia in terms of city scale and streetscapes. They stated that they were returning home with a renewed interest in making changes at home and valuing the positive features of the city. So when asked »What can your home city learn from Barcelona?« the Sofia group chose an image of a woman cleaning the pavement with a mop.

»My summary is to learn to love the city and to do the best for our city, to work and to be proud of the city. She is cleaning the streets, it is very important for us to love our city, to work for our city and to be part of our city, to feel good in the city.« (Niki, Workshop Participant)

The Sofia group also reflected on the opportunities for change in Sofia, a city which is relatively new in the European community; they were critical of the levels of traffic and pollution in the city due to the availability of credit and an associated high growth in car ownership. The group chose an image of a bicycle.

»I have learned that our ways are open and we have many op-portunities and we have to use them,« a young woman reflected on an aspect of Bulgarian culture. While walking the streets of Barcelona she heard what she felt to be very typical Bulgari-an music being played in a public square. She ran over to lis-ten to this music as it reminded her of home. Like many Bul-garians, she percieved gypsies as a negative aspect of daily life, prior to leaving Bulgaria. However, since travelling, she finds their music and culture typically Bulgarian. As she stated in an interview:

> *»They remind me of home because they are everywhere. [...] I never really liked Sofia so much, but every time I come back it is a little bit more real and something to rediscover«.* (Kalina, Workshop Participant)

Much of the discussion in the groups reflected on the value of friendship, comparing the friendliness in Barcelona with the attitudes of people in their home cities. As this London parti-cipant stated, »I think our home city could learn to be more friendly from Barcelona. In London people just keep themselves to themselves. I think people in London could learn more to work as a team; they are not as friendly as people in other countries. I think we could learn to have more respect for peo-ple who come from other countries as well as people who live there.« (Becky, London)

The London participants were impressed with the openness and friendliness they encountered on a visit to a Barcelona school in Trinitat Vella.

> *»When we went into the school, probably in London the most that would happen is you would just have a bunch of people looking at you, staring at you, wondering ›Who are they?‹ ›What are they here to do?‹ But here we just come to a school and straight away everyone is talking to us. They want to know who we are. I met quite a lot of people and they are all my friends now, we went there again and we were all talking, and I just asked them to play football and we all started playing football together. It was really nice, just communicating with a lot of people; it feels good like you know I have got Spanish friends now.«* (Chirag, Workshop Participant)

While these can be read as fairly straightforward comments about the value of friendship, the participants reflected on the ways that they had embodied some of the unfriendly attitudes that they had described; they reflected on the pressures that they were experiencing at home where the messages that they regularly heard were »stay off the streets or you might get robbed.« In particular, the young people from London were impressed by the openness of the school children of their age that they had met when doing workshops at a school in Trinitat Vella. After arriving and being a little nervous, the London youth were quickly trying to converse in Spanish and Catalan, playing football, listening to each other's music, and swapping phone numbers and e-mail addresses.

The LAB2 workshops were also valuable opportunities to explore the ways in which photography can be used to over-come problems of verbal and written communication. The artist Oliver Walker's »Copy Me« game was an interesting explora-tion of the potentials of photography as a form of visual com-munication; the project stimulates reflection on urban sur-roundings by playfully comparing pictures. The participants all began with photographs of some flowers seen through a shop or restaurant window, with reflections of the street scene on the glass and glimpses into the interior of the image. Partici-pants were asked to copy this image, whether through the form, the feeling, colours, shapes, or structure of the original. This prompted them to reflect on the image and be inventive in their interpretation. The participants will continue this exercise in their home cities via the Citipix website stripe function, thereby drawing attention to global proximity through modern commu-nication media. Photography was used effectively and playful-ly. During the visit to the school in Trinitat Vella the participants played a game of »photographic paintball« that required them to chase each other around the playground to capture a face shot at close range of another participant. The winner was the one with the most captured shots.

On a more everyday level, photography facilitated commu-nication across the group. Young people with a wide range of languages used photographs to communicate with each other, describing what was in the photo in several languages. The cam-era enables intrapersonal communication, just through the sim-ple act of asking »Can I take your photo?« and the answer to the question »Why do you want to take my photo?« or being seen in the street and being approached and asked »Why they are taking photographs?«

LEGACIES

This Signs of the City exhibition and conference phase of the project solidified the European dimensions of the project, par-ticularly the EU Culture programme's aim to promote the trans-national mobility of cultural players and to encourage the trans-national circulation of works and cultural and artistic products. The constellation of cultural players that it brought together was both a strength and a challenge for the project in terms of its ambitious scale, its short timescale, and its individual part-ner's capacities to deliver the project whilst still meeting its

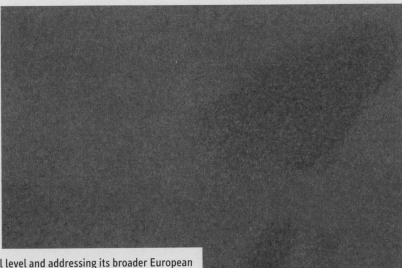

The pictures are film stills from the film project »Flocking«, filmed in Rome January 2008, an interdisciplinary collaboration between HfG Karlsruhe University of Arts and Design and Starflag project, Center for Statistical Mechanics and Complexity (SMC) of CNR-INFM Rome
by Ulrike Barwanietz, Maša Bušic, Irene Giardina, Herwig Hoffmann, Johanna Hoth, Giuseppe Ielasi Samuel Korn, Armin Linke Renato Rinaldi and Marc Teuscher
co-produced by HfG Karlsruhe University of Art and Design, Goethe-Institute Italy, ZKM Center for Art and Media Karlsruhe and Akademie der Künste Berlin

demands at a local level and addressing its broader European aims. At the close of the project the diverse range of expertise and agendas that each of these partners brought, contributed to a rich mix of perspectives, aspirations, and professional expertise, which crossed disciplinary, sectoral and national, boundaries. The final Signs of the City conferences and exhibitions have proven to be valuable opportunities for the participants and artists from each of the cities to meet, work together, reflect on their practice within a wider European creative and artistic sector, and to debate on the challenges of contemporary urbanism. At its close the project's legacies include Europe- and city-wide networks of artists and arts organisations that are keen to develop and build on the working relationships and project concerns such as citizenship and the potential of participatory arts and new media, which the project enabled. Participating organisations have already developed new project and funding applications to take this work forward, furthering the potential to use photography and new technologies in exploring young people's experience of citizenship and their rights to the city. In unison, the exhibitions and conferences have synthesised the participatory process, aesthetic outcomes and intellectual significance of the project. At its most powerful, the sort of work that has been produced through the project reflects both photographic excellence and a profoundly ethical engagement with issues of citizenship, belonging, and *la droit a la ville* (the right to the city), themes profoundly relevant to arts work taking place at the fortieth anniversary of les événements of 1968.

Acknowledgements

For their commitment and contributions to the project, we would like to thank:

ORGANISERS

Aliénor Dauchez, urban dialogues, Berlin
Britt Hatzius, urban dialogues, London
Carme Romero, Hangar, Barcelona
Carolin Berendts, Next Interkulturelle Projekte, Berlin
Dr. Alison Rooke, CUCR Goldsmiths College, University of London
Dr. Bernd Scherer, Haus der Kulturen der Welt, Berlin
Felix Getzmann, urban dialogues, Berlin
Heidi Walter, urban dialogues, Berlin
Henrike Grohs, Next Interkulturelle Projekte, Berlin
Ignacio Somovila, Hangar, Barcelona
Ilze Black, Watermans, London
Inga Seidler, urban dialogues, Berlin
Jan Lennox, Watermans, London

Javier Rodrigo, ArtiBarri, Barcelona
Jessica Glause, urban dialogues, Berlin
Meike von Appen, Zukunftsbau, Berlin
Michael Raj Kunsmann, urban dialogues, Berlin
Milkana Lazarova, Atelier for Free Associations, Sofia
Oliver Kummer, urban dialogues, Berlin
Pedro Soler, Hangar, Barcelona
Prof. Michael Keith, CUCR Goldsmiths College, University of London
Sabine Klippstein, Zukunftsbau, Berlin
Sibylle Kraut-Eppich, urban dialogues, Berlin
Uta Staiger, urban dialogues, London
Velislava Donkin, Atelier for Free Associations, Sofia
Xavi Perez, ArtiBarri, Barcelona

COMMUNICATION

anschlaege.de, Berlin
Michael Aichler, mediacluster, Stuttgart
Michael Tizzano, mediacluster, Stuttgart
Oliver Kremershof, urban dialogues, Berlin
Robert Brommer, urban dialogues, Berlin
Sally Below, sally below cultural affairs, Berlin

INSTITUTIONS

Björn Fricke, Sony Deutschland GmbH
Centre for Creative Communities, London
Cultural Contact Point, Bonn
Dr. Elke Ritt, British Council Berlin
Dr. Rudolf Bartsch, Goethe Institute Bulgaria
Eugenio Delfino, European Commission Brussels
Guido Jansen, British Council Berlin
Interarts Foundation, Barcelona
Itziar Taboada, Spanish Embassy Berlin
Kai Fischer, Sony Deutschland GmbH
Karl Pfeiffer, Goethe Institute London
Ursula Wahl, Goethe Institute Barcelona

ARTISTS

Almendra Salazar, Barcelona
Andréas Lang, München
Andrei Rashev, Sofia
Diego Ferrari, London
Douglas Nicolson, London
Erica Scourti, London
Harriet Murray, London
Ivan Kiuranov, Sofia
Javier Oliden, Barcelona
Jörg Metzner, Berlin
Jürgen Kuhn, Berlin
Mapi Arramendia, Barcelona
Martin Ruge, Berlin
Mathu Seichter, Kiel
Melissa Bliss, London
Monica Segura-Marquez, Berlin
Neil Taylor, London
Nuria Calafell, Barcelona
Oliver Walker, Liverpool
Pamela Gallo, Barcelona
Paula Kleiman, Barcelona
Terez Osztafi, London

Photo Credits

INTRODUCTION

Signs of the City – Metropolis Speaking | 9–13
urban dialogues, Stefan Horn and Martin Ruge

WORKSHOPS

Campbell Works | 26–29
Artists: Neil Taylor and Harriet Murray / Campbell Works London
Photographers published: Sophia Mushold (Sophia) p 27,
Anna Seidorova (AnnaS), Michael O'Mahony (BlackyCrazyKill),
Ilja Khenkine (BryonX), Lisa Simon (LisaS), Robert Schröder
(Rober), Sebastian Kalbus (Sebastian), Sophia Mushold
(Sophia), Thomas Olm (Thomas), Neil Taylor, Harriet Murray

The Barcelona Experience | 30–35
Artists: Nuria Calafell / Teleduca, Almendra Salazar, Mapi
Aramendia / mapi, Paula Kleiman / Teleduca, Pamela Gallo /
UbuTV, Javier Oliden / UbuTV, Javier Rodrigo / TEB.
Photographers published: Samuel Comas (samuel) p 31, Clara
Rosell (Clara Rosell), Natasha Estrada Urán (Natasha),
Lucas Rodríguez (Lucas Rodríguez), Laura Vives (Laura Vives),
Johanna Jimenez (joana), Samuel Comas (samuel), Kelvon de
Leon (vienkle), Camino Simarro (kimno), Mireia Acien (Mireia
Acien), Diane Rose Aguilar (enaid), Bibekanand Dey (bibek),
Adrian Cortes Lorenzo (Adrian), Gulam Farred (gulam),
Waqas Ahmined (Waqas), Shahnawaz Mohamed (Shahnawaz),
Ester Garcia (ester)

Construct your own Sign | 36–39
Artist: Diego Ferrari
Photographers published: Keynan Dietrich (Keynan) p 37,
Antonella Palmowski (Antonella), Magareta von Oswald
(Magareta), Oliver Kummer (oliver)

Walking, Talking, Photographing | 40–43
Artist: Melissa Bliss
Photographers published: Melissa Bliss p 41, Mozzam Ghazi
(the star 1000), Craig Gibbs (motormania), Jarryd Kent (jarryd),
Uriel Blackwood (uriel)

London East | 44–47
Artist: Douglas Nicolson / SPACE Studios
Photographers published: Douglas Nicolson p 45, Chevonnie
Dennis (arsenal), Cato Heath (Cheath), Cheryl Bowen (chez),
Elliot Ojuri (elliott), Erik Bischop (ErikLB), Georgia Elander
(Gigi77), Hadrian Douglas-Johuson (hadriandj), Melanie Yugo
(Myugo), Dienga Difika (RoboD3000), Shamina Begum
(Shamina.begum), Shaniq, Toby Plowman (Tboandfshady),
Michael Ojuri (Toxic kid), Sarra Said-Wardell (Sarra), Gloire
Ammany (McGloire)

Map of Signs | 48–51
Artist: Martin Ruge
Photographers published: Patrick Dzieblinski p 49, agund,
Dominik Wolfram (domken), dumme, Tahsin Özkan (jason),
Benjamin-Pascal Buhler (on-city.com), Sebastian Meister (seba),
Patrick Dzieblinski (shady_89), stefan, Valentin Burkhardt
(valentin_burkhardt)

Freestyle Berlin | 52–55
Artists: Stefan Horn and Britt Hatzius
Photographers published: Michael Klaus p 53, Johanna Richter
(MS Hanna), Anna Kley, Sarah Ramirez (sua), Sandra Gonzales
Leal (Virgin-Superstar), Lucien Gulak (lucien), Oliver Kummer
(oliver), Christopher Buckendahl (dschiesis), Sofie Müller
(sofie), Felix Getzmann (fg1311), Hedwig Haukler (hedi),
Marcus Spiller (M.S.)

The Young People and their Place in the City –
Point Of View And History | 56–59
Artists: Ivan Kiuranov and Andrey Rashev
Photographers published: Ivan Manchev (Manchev) p 57,
Andrey Nikolov (andrei), Kalina Tekelieva (kalina), Lilio Petkova
(lili), Marta Pesheva (marta), Galina Balezdrova (smashy),
Boian Tepavicharov (bobbyfuego), Ivaylo Petrov (drksrrw),
Tzvetelina Ivanova (flowerline), Maxim Nenkov (Maxim),
Iva Nova (metratonic), Vera Nickolaeva (ninek), Zlatoena
Gocheva (zlatinka)

LAB 2 – BARCELONA | 61–70

Photographers published: Zlatoena Gocheva (zlatinka),
Ivan Manchev (manchev), Marta Pesheva (marta), Kalina
Teckelieva (kalina), Nickola Belchev (niki), Oliver Kummer
(oliver), Antonella Palmowski (antonella), Michaela
Görlitz (michi), Tahsin Özkan (Jason), Dominik Wolfram
(domken), Ajoke Alade (ajoke), Hodo Ali-Abyan (hodo),

Rebecca Lynn Swinton-Bland (rebecca), Chirag Sachania (chirag), Omar Amal Carby (omar), Clara Rosell (Clara Rosell), Natasha Estrada Urán (Natasha), Lucas Rodríguez (Lucas Rodríguez), Laura Vives (Laura Vives), Jhoanna Jimenez (joana), Samuel Comas (samuel), Kelvon de Leon (vienkle), Camino Simarro (kimno), Mireia Acien (Mireia Acien), Diane Rose Aguilar (enaid), Bibekanand Dey (bibek), Adrian Cortes Lorenzo (Adrian), Gulam Farred (gulam), Waqas Ahmined (Waqas), Shahnawaz Mohamed (Shahnawaz), Ester Garcia (ester)

Exhibitions |71–80

Andrei Rashev, Douglas Nicolson, Keynan Dietrich, Stefan Horn, Watermans London

Pictures |81–144

Annika Petersohn (anni/ka/tze) 137 bottom, 141 top
Antonella Palmowski (Antonella) 100, 112 bottom, 113 top, 133
Bibekanand Dey (bibek) 111 bottom
Boian Tepavicharov (bobbyfuego) 106 bottom
Camino Simarro (kmino) 84, 117 bottom, 121 top
Chris B. (dschiesis) 128, 129
Christin Renner (tini) 99 bottom
Clara Rosell (Clara Rosell) 123 top
Darja Ameltchenko (Darja) 85
Dominik Wolfram (domken) 114 bottom
Ester Garcia (ester) 134 bottom
evil lurks 135 bottom
Galina Balezdrova (smashy) 104 bottom
Ilja Khenkine (BryonX) 95 bottom, 125 top, 130 bottom, 131 bottom
Irida Dalla (Iris) 98 bottom
Iva Nova (metratonic) 139
Ivan Parvanov (IParvanov) 118 top, 119 bottom
Ivaylo Petrov (drksrrw) 92, 93, 120
Jahangir Miah (Jahangir) 105 bottom
Jarryd Kent (jarryd) 124 bottom
Kalina Tekelieva (KALINA) 122 bottom
Katharina Kendzia (Kathi) 86, 87, 125 bottom
Kelvin de Leon (vienkle) 121 bottom
Kristina Gospodinova (krisi) 94, 95 top
Laura Vives (Laura Vives) 110 top
Lucien Gulak (Lucien) 136 bottom, 137 top

Margareta Margareta (Margareta) 102
Marta Pesheva (marta) 132
Maxim Nenkov (Maxim) 115
Maximilian Stauss (Maxx) 130 bottom
Natasha Estrada Urán (Natasha) 97 bottom
Nuria Arias (nuria) 140 bottom
Raq petrova (Raaq) 82 bottom, 83, 126
Sandra Gonzalez (Virgin-Superstar) 112 top, 113 bottom, 116
Sarah Ramirez (sua) 101, 104 top, 108, 109, 140 top
Sebastian Kalbus 91 bottom
Sebastian Meister (Seba) 123 bottom
Shamina Begum (Shamina.begum) 118 bottom
Sinthuja Srikumar (sinthu) 90 top, 96 bottom, 130 top
Sofie Müller (sofie) 103
Teddy Borisova (therainbow) 82 top, 107, 117 top, 127, 131 top
Toby Plowman (Tboandfshady) 99 top
Tzvetelina Ivanova (flowerline) 105 top, 124 top
Vera Nickolaeva (ninek) 91 top, 110 bottom, 111 top, 119 top, 134 top, 138, 141 bottom
Waqas Ahmined (Waqas) 114 top
Zlatoena Gocheva (zlatinka) 88, 89, 90 bottom, 96 top, 97 top, 106 top, 122 top, 135 top, 136 top, 142, 143

Conference

Signs, my City, Dialogues |146–148
Aroa Cortes Lorenzo (bomboncito_cali), Veronica Comas (veronica), Andreu Romani (andreu), Laura Vives (Laura Vives)

Attention! |149–151
Dominik Wolfram (domken)

The Subjective Side of the Objective |152–154
Hedwig Haukler (Hedi), Manol Donchev (manoldonchev), Zlatoena G. (Zlatinka), Christopher Corgiat: World Statue (fotolia.com), Wiesiek Zieba: Legs in Stockings (fotolia.com), Antonella Palmowski (Antonella)

Imprint

Signs of the City – Metropolis Speaking is initiated and organised by Berlin-based metropolitan art organisation urban dialogues.

urban dialogues
Bergstr. 71
D-10115 Berlin
Tel: +49 - (0)30 - 469 96 39 0
mail@urbandialogues.de
www.urbandialogues.de

House of World Cultures

John-Foster-Dulles-Allee 10
D-10557 Berlin
Tel. + 49 - (0)30 - 397 87 0
info@hkw.de
www.hkw.de
The House of World Cultures is supported by the State Minister at the Federal Chancellery for Culture and Media and by the Federal Foreign Office.

 Der Beauftragte der Bundesregierung für Kultur und Medien   Auswärtiges Amt

Signs of the City – Metropolis Speaking is co-organised by:

   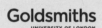

Signs of the City – Metropolis Speaking is supported by:

With the support of the
Culture Programme of the European Union

 Education and Culture DG

This project has been funded with support from the European Commission. This publication reflects the views only of the author, and the Commission cannot be held responsible for any use which may be made of the information contained therein.

© 2009 by JOVIS Verlag GmbH
Texts by kind permission of the authors.
Pictures by kind permission of the photographer/holders of the picture rights. All rights reserved.
Cover: anschlaege.de, Berlin
Editing: Stefan Horn, Rudolf Netzelmann, Peter Winkels
Co-Editing: Britt Hatzius, Inga Seidler, Uta Staiger
Design and setting: anschlaege.de, Berlin
Lithography: anschlaege.de, Berlin
Printing and binding: Grafisches Centrum Cuno GmbH
Bibliographic information published by Die Deutsche Bibliothek
Die Deutsche Bibliothek lists this publication in the Deutsche Nationalbibliografie; detailed bibliographic data are available on the Internet at http://dnb.ddb.de
ISBN: 978-3-86859-014-2

JOVIS Verlag GmbH
Kurfürstenstraße 15/16
10785 Berlin
www.jovis.de